AF333259

THE CHAMPION INSIDE

THE CHAMPION INSIDE

The Story of a Young Rider's Pursuit of Her Dreams and Her Belief in the Horse She Loved

by
Alyxandra Swanhall

Aventine Press

Cover photo – Copyright © Roger Ratzenberger Photography

© 2008, Alyxandra Swanhall
First Edition

Without limiting the rights under copyright reserved above,
no part of this publication may be reproduced, stored in or introduced into a retrieval system, or transmitted, in any form or by any means (electronic, mechanical, photocopying, recording, or otherwise), without the prior written permission of both the copyright owner and the publisher of this book.

Published by Aventine Press
750 State St. #319
San Diego CA, 92101

ISBN: 1-59330-558-3

Printed in the United States of America
ALL RIGHTS RESERVED

For my mom and dad.

TABLE OF CONTENTS

Preface

Although I am only sixteen, I have had the opportunity to work with numerous people in the equine industry since beginning my journey with horses at age three. Each one of them, in their own way, has helped me to become a more knowledgeable horseperson, an accomplished rider, and what I believe, a better person in general. I thank all of them for the lessons they've taught me and the experiences we've shared; without them I would not have been able to achieve my goals. In an effort to protect the privacy of some of individuals, I have purposely either not referred to them by name or have changed their name. I have done so in fairness to them because although my story is a narrative of actual events, it is presented solely from my perspective.

It is my greatest hope that my experiences will inspire other young riders to pursue their equestrian dreams even if they don't have the most expensive horse, work with a renowned trainer, or have large financial resources. I sincerely believe that by pursuing your goals with integrity, passion, determination, perseverance, and hard work, your dreams can become reality.

Acknowledgments

There are three very special people in my life who were instrumental in helping me throughout my equestrian endeavors and during the writing of this book; they are my heroes:

Vicky West, whom I have known for most of my life, has been a wonderful friend and mentor. Whether helping me look for and "test drive" a new horse, fixing a behavioral problem or teaching me training techniques, she has always generously shared her time, insight and expertise with me. Whenever I doubted my abilities, be it riding or writing, her response was always the same, "Girl, don't worry. You got it goin' on!" When I would express concerns about comments directed at my horse, she would tell me, "Leave Jay alone, he's fine." She always believed in both of us from day one.

Cheryl and Dennis, my amazing parents, who have always given me their love and unconditional support my entire life. They have unselfishly made many sacrifices over the years so I could pursue my dreams.

My dad has spent hours helping with my chores and taking care of my pets so I could attend horseshows, practice, work on my book, and do my schoolwork. While he doesn't always get the recognition he deserves as he quietly supports me at home, his efforts have provided me with the many hours I needed to focus on my goals.

And most notably my mom, whose only hope had been that I would like horses enough to trail ride with her; I think she got a little more than she bargained for. She entered a world she was completely unfamiliar with, yet she was determined to do whatever was necessary to help me succeed. Over time, she became my trainer, strategist, confidant, groom, horse hauler, and so much more. She has selflessly committed countless hours of her time and has always been resolute in her pursuit to find answers. I attribute most of my success as a rider to her unwavering belief in me and never-ending encouragement.

It was my mom who suggested I document my journey with Jay when I first began competing in medal classes. Although we had found numerous fictional stories of young equestrians who had overcome obstacles to achieve success in the ring, we were never able to find any actual accounts on the subject written by junior riders. She felt I might have an interesting tale to tell if, like the riders in the novels, Jay and I were successful. I never could have imagined at the time what an unbelievable journey it would turn out to be. I will always be grateful to her for guiding me down this path. She is truly an inspiration.

INTRODUCTION

2007 Marshall and Sterling Children's Horse Medal Final

September 16, 2007

As I sit atop my horse facing the Grand Prix ring before me, I feel a fluttering in my stomach as the excitement of the moment overtakes me. Jay and I are preparing to enter the ring for the 2007 Marshall and Sterling Children's Horse Medal Finals. I remember standing up on the hillside that surrounds the arena last year watching the riders take their turns during the 2006 Finals. It was at that moment I knew I was going to be one of them this year.

No matter what happened in the coming moments, I knew Jay and I were already winners. My partnership with him had begun shortly after one of the most devastating events of my life; and this was the culmination of over two and a half years of determination, hard work, setbacks, tears, elation, and every emotion imaginable. Although our journey had been fraught with some disappointments along the way, we had refused to be defeated by them. We conquered each adversity that came our way together, which made our triumphs all the more meaningful. Among other things, they had taught me to never give up on my dreams, regardless of how overwhelming the obstacles facing me seemed. It also proved that "backyard" riders like me really could achieve their dreams of success and make it to a national equitation final.

Most importantly though, I had developed a bond with my horse that was stronger than any I could have ever imagined. Time and again Jay had shown me how much heart he had, proving repeatedly that he was willing to trust me even when he was nervous or insecure. I especially loved those moments when we were completely in tune with each other and it actually seemed as though our minds were one. There would be an almost lyrical quality to our movements as we maneuvered around a course of jumps. It was as if we were dancers moving in perfect unison with each other, both knowing what the other's next step would be.

My reverie is broken as I notice that the rider in the ring has finished her course and is moving toward me. Now it is my turn, and time to focus on the task at hand. I take a deep breath and enter the ring…

CHAPTER 1

Discovering the Wonderful World of Horses

I really can't remember a time when we didn't have horses, although I was already three when my mom bought her first one. She had been horse crazy from the time she was a little girl, but her family had never been able to afford one. She and my dad both worked and they had finally reached a point where she had the financial means to buy and care for her own horse. Finally her childhood dream came true when, at thirty-three years old, she bought a six year old registered Paint horse named Tardy Chief for $2,500. My mom had fallen in love with him the minute she saw him and had renamed him Cheyenne. Although he had some major issues as a result of being abused, she saw past that, and in time he became a loving member of our family and an incredible trail horse that she could ride virtually anywhere.

For the first couple of years she boarded him at a local barn, and I remember hanging out with the other kids while she rode. After about six months I decided I was tired of watching everyone else ride and asked if I could take lessons. Although my mom would sometimes lead me around on her horse, it wasn't until I sat in the saddle for my first lesson that I truly fell in love with riding.

After several months of learning the basics, my trainer suggested that I attend a local farm show with the rest of the barn kids. As soon as my mom mentioned the possibility of going to a show, I was immediately ready to pack my things, jump in the car and go. I was so excited when we went to the store to buy my new show clothes that I could barely contain myself while trying them on.

In October 1995, I rode in my first horse show. I was entered in the leadline class and one of the older girls at the barn offered to take me into the ring on her horse. There I was, 4 years old, sitting atop a 16.2 hand bay Thoroughbred named *Palimest*. My legs were so short they had to wrap the stirrup leathers around the irons repeatedly so I could place my feet in them properly. My hands were so tiny I could barely wrap them around the reins. I still love looking at the photo of myself sitting so straight in the saddle with a very focused, serious look on my face as I waited for my class. I went into the ring that day determined to remember everything my trainer had told me. When it was over and the ring person handed me my very first ribbon, the horse show bug bit me.

During the next year, I continued to show in leadline and eventually walk classes at local shows. I was having a great time riding the barn owner's aged Quarter Horse mare and my lessons were progressing nicely. Just as I was ready to move up to walk/trot, the owner decided the mare was being used too much for lessons and without warning pulled her from the program. One of the young boarders kindly offered to let my trainer use her pony for lessons. Unfortunately, the change didn't work out very well for me. Because I wasn't strong enough to get the pony to move forward with just my legs, my trainer gave me a riding crop. For the next three lessons all she did was yell repeatedly, "Hit that pony. Beat that pony. Make that pony go." I absolutely hated it and told my parents I didn't want to take lessons anymore. They offered to find another trainer or buy me a pony of my own, but I had already made up my mind. I knew my mom was disappointed for me, but she realized I mentally needed to take a break. She was definitely happy though when I told her I still wanted to trail ride.

On several occasions I had accompanied my mom when she rode with some friends in a nearby town called St. Cloud. Since we only had one horse, one of the women let me ride her teenaged son's mule, Bocephus. The first time I rode him she assured us that he would be the perfect babysitter for me; and she was right. It was amazing how seriously Bo took his job of keeping me safe no matter what we encountered on the trail or how the horses we rode with behaved. Nothing flustered him. He seemed to know exactly where I was and what I was doing at all times. He would not cross a road with me until one of the adults gave him the okay and never increased his speed unless I asked him to. It was quite an interesting experience for my mom and me since we'd never been around mules before and had no idea how truly intelligent they were. And to top it off, from the first time they met, Cheyenne and Bo acted as if they had known each other all their lives and were best friends.

There's one trail ride in particular I'll never forget. In order to reach our destination, the horses had to cross a very steep ditch which was about ten feet deep on either side. I was five at the time and for some reason the thought of going down into the ditch terrified me. As I watched some of the other horses and riders maneuver down one side of the bank and up the other, my anxiety got the better of me. Several times I started to dismount, got halfway off Bo, then changed my mind and sat back in the saddle. Thankfully, he put up with all drama and just stood there quietly.

Finally, my mom said I had to make a decision; either stay on Bo and ride down the ditch or get off and walk. In a panic I started crying, tried to dismount, slipped, and fell right under Bo's belly. There was a collective gasp among the adults as I hit the ground, but Bo didn't move a muscle. I quickly rolled out from underneath him and stood next to him shaking. He turned his head to look back at me, made sure I was clear, and then proceeded to walk down one side of the ditch and up the other. Once he reached the other side, he stood calmly waiting for me. I proceeded to scramble down the side of the ditch, jump over the little stream at the bottom, and climb up the opposite side. When I reached Bo, I hopped back on and we finished our ride.

In July of 1997, my mom received a surprising call from Bo's owner. Due to an unexpected family situation they were going to have to sell him. She asked if we would be interested in buying him since I seemed to like him so much. Within the hour we were driving to her house to pick him up. His owner had told us he was fourteen, but my mom suspected he was a bit older than that. When our equine dentist had a chance to look at him, he said he would be generous saying he was seventeen. He was actually probably older than that, but it didn't really matter because I loved him to pieces. My mom always told everyone it was the best $1,000 she ever spent; Bo always took care of me and was definitely worth that amount a hundred times over.

Periodically she would ask me if I wanted to take riding lessons again, but I always said I wasn't interested. At the time I was perfectly content going on trail rides with Bo. "Besides," I would tell her, "I only rode mules, not horses."

That presented an interesting problem when we went on vacation in March of 1999. My mom really wanted to go riding in the mountains with my dad and me, but knew I wouldn't get on a strange horse. After researching nearly every stable in the area, she found the only one that had a mule. When she called to make our reservations she explained my situation. They assured her they would "reserve" the mule for me.

When I first met Nui, I was a bit intimidated by the 16.1 hand gelding, considering he was quite a bit larger than our little 13.3 hand Bo. Once I overcame my initial fear though and was securely seated in the saddle, it was a completely different story. Since Nui was larger than most of the horses on the line, I towered over everyone else, including my parents. I quickly sensed that his "mule brain" was engaged, which allowed me to relax and enjoy the ride. Of course, I had an absolutely wonderful time riding him through the mountains and my parents had to pry me away from him when we returned to the barn.

That vacation proved to be a turning point for me when it came to riding. I'd had so much fun riding in the mountains that shortly after returning home I asked my mom if it would be okay if I took lessons again. She was very happy about my decision and promised to find the perfect person to train me.

It didn't take long for my mom to find the promised riding instructor to get me started again. Miss Phyllis owned her own stable about twenty minutes from our house and was recommended by one of the women my mom worked with. For years she had bred, raised and shown champion Tennessee Walking horses. Now the jovial, hard-working grandmother spent her time giving riding lessons to youngsters. I was immediately drawn to her cheerful and warm personality. Miss Phyllis introduced me to an aged pony named Cinnamon who just happened to be the same color, and almost the same size, as Bo. He was exactly what I needed.

Soon my friend Shelby began taking lessons with me every Saturday morning. We spent our time maneuvering around obstacles and ground poles and circling the ring at the walk, trot and canter. Occasionally, we would get to ride around Miss Phyllis' property on a trail ride. It was the perfect scenario and I loved every minute of it.

CHAPTER 2

A Pony of My Own

In the winter of 1999, my parents purchased five acres of land in west central Florida. They decided that it would be more economical in the long run to take care of our horses ourselves, rather than keep boarding them. As construction began on our new house and barn that summer, we sold the house we were living in and temporarily rented one near our new property. Since it was closer to Miss Phyllis' farm than our other barn, my mom decided it would be more convenient for us to move Cheyenne and Bo to her place while our house was being built.

During that same time, my mom had begun to search for the perfect horse or pony for me. Over the course of six months we looked at dozens of potential mounts in all shapes and sizes. We even brought a few home on trial, but each time we sent them back due to health or attitude issues. My mom had become very frustrated at her inability to find a horse for me and wondered if she'd ever find something suitable.

One afternoon in November she was checking the Internet and found an ad that had just been placed for a large 8-year-old child-friendly pony named Tic Toc that was listed for $5,000. It said he was located in a town outside of Ocala called Summerfield. After making arrangements to see him, my mom explained to me that she was tired of looking at horses and if Tic Toc didn't work out, he would be the last horse she'd look at until after Christmas. He seemed promising, so I kept my fingers crossed.

She'd invited her friend Vicky to join us on our quest so she could make sure he was kid-safe. My mom had met Vicky several years earlier when she moved from Pennsylvania to Florida and boarded her horse at the same barn as Cheyenne. Her mother was a horse trainer who also bred sporthorses; therefore, Vicky had been around them all her life and was very knowledgeable.

The weird thing was we hadn't seen or heard from Vicky for several years since we had all moved our horses to new facilities. A few days before we were supposed to check Tic Toc out, my mom was walking through the break room at work and saw Vicky sitting at a table. Neither of them realized the other was working for the same company. Naturally, they started talking about horses and my mom told her about our mission to find a horse for me. After filling her in on the list of rejects, she asked Vicky if she'd like to join us when we went to see Tic Toc. Since she didn't have anything planned, she eagerly agreed to go with us and test drive him.

A few days later, my mom, Vicky and I headed to Summerfield to check out Tic Toc. When we arrived at the farm where he was supposed to be, we couldn't see a horse in the pasture and no one seemed to be home. As we glanced across the street to another house, we noticed a red roan pony grazing in the front yard. The ad had mentioned something about him having a red roan patch on his side, so we thought that might be him.

After we parked the car near the seemingly empty pasture and got out, Tic Toc saw us, walked out of the trees and over to the fence. I couldn't believe how cute and friendly he was! Vicky climbed through the fence into the pasture and started doing some of her kid-proofing tests; he passed them all with flying colors. A short time later, the woman who was selling him arrived home with her daughter, who happened to be just a few years older than me. Once they started talking to the woman, my mom and Vicky felt she was extremely forthcoming and honest about Tic Toc. She said she was selling him for a friend and that her daughter had been riding him while he was staying at their place. After the girl rode him around a side pasture and Vicky took him for a test drive, I got my chance to ride him. I knew immediately we'd finally found "the one." Vicky worked with my mom on getting a good price for him and the owners eventually agreed on $3,500. They wanted him to go to a family and were willing to reduce the price to ensure he went to a good home. After passing his vet check, we moved Ticky to Miss Phyllis' farm.

Shortly thereafter, my mom hired Vicky to work in her department, and she has stayed with her to this day. In the years that followed she would become the one person aside from my parents that I could always rely on for help, especially where horses were concerned. Whenever my mom would mention I was having an issue with one of our horses, Vicky was on it. There have been many times she's changed her own plans to come out to our house after work or on a weekend to help me out. On the few occasions when she wasn't entirely sure how to fix a problem, behavior, or illness, she was able to reach out to her extensive network of contacts to find a solution. I have always sincerely appreciated everything she has done for me over the years.

Finally, in March 2000, our own barn was finished and we moved "the boys" to their new home. The following month my mom, dad and I moved into our house. One of the best parts about our new house was that there were acres and acres of orange groves around us that we could trail ride through. On the other side of the groves were a nature preserve and a beautiful lake. Nestled among a wooded area that separated the groves was a small cemetery that we assumed belonged to the family that had previously owned the property. Most of the markers had dates from the late 1800's to the mid-1900's. I used to love bringing flowers with me on our trail rides so I could show my respect and leave them near the headstones.

Back then we would spend hours riding around the area, and I was constantly amazed at all the wildlife we would see. There were birds of every kind; from songbirds, like mockingbirds and bluebirds, to water birds, like snowy egrets and great blue herons. My favorites though were the birds of prey that lived around the lake. There were kestrels, red-tailed hawks, swallow-tailed kites, ospreys, and even a pair of magnificent bald eagles who nested in the nature preserve every year. In addition to the wide variety of birds, we would also see rabbits, tortoises, turtles, armadillos, raccoons, and foxes; snakes of all sizes and colors; and even the occasional shy coyote or bobcat.

Of course, since we were in Florida and riding around a lake, we would inevitably run into an alligator from time to time. They were the only critters that really scared me, especially the big ones. One time when the lake was low because of a severe drought, we came across a gator that we guessed had to be at least thirteen or fourteen feet long laying on the dried up lake bed next to a shallow pool of water. He was huge, and I was scared to death! We tried to give him a wide berth as we rode around the edge of the lake; not wanting to become gator bait simply because his normal food supply had almost disappeared. As we came around behind him, he must have heard the horses. It was astonishing how quickly he was able to scramble into the water, where he started rolling and thrashing like crazy. I had to admit I couldn't wait to get as far away from that big guy as possible!

One of our favorite rituals at the time was watching the Grand Prix competitions every Sunday on OLN. It didn't take long for me to become a huge fan of Margie Engle. I was very impressed with her riding skills and determination, and especially loved watching her compete on her amazing horse, Perin. Some of my other favorite riders were Beezie Madden, Richard Spooner, Leslie Howard, and Ludger Beerbaum. I loved the name of Ludger's horse, Gladys S, because that was my grandmother's name. I think watching those talented riders navigate thrilling jumper courses each week was what sparked a desire in me to want to show again.

I was really enjoying having my own pony at home and being able to spend time with him every day, but I wanted to do something more challenging with him. I soon began hinting that I'd like to learn how to jump and start showing again. While Miss Phyllis had provided me with a wonderful foundation, she was no longer interested in showing and had no experience in jumping. Although I would miss seeing her every weekend for lessons, I knew it was time to move on.

The hard part was going to be finding a barn that would allow us to trailer Ticky in each week for lessons. Having only really been exposed to low key "pleasure-type" barns, it didn't take long for my mom and I to realize how naïve we were when it came to hunter/jumper barns and the world of showing.

Over the next several years, I ended up riding with three different barns. The first was a locally competitive barn that was run by a woman named Linda who was trying to build up her relatively new business. She was very accommodating and said we could trailer Ticky in for lessons, but asked that we leave him there for a month so the "pony trainer" could work with him. Ticky knew his job and had a lot of show miles on him; therefore, leaving him at the barn was not necessary and limited the time I could spend riding him. Since we knew we wouldn't be keeping him there permanently, and to provide them with an understanding of what he could do, my mom reluctantly agreed to leave him there. At the end of the month, the trainer insisted that he wasn't ready and needed another month's work. My mom agreed to two more weeks, but told her that was it. Whatever work he needed, we could do it ourselves at home.

We quickly discovered that there seemed to be a revolving door of trainers at the barn. Just when I would get used to working with one trainer, they would leave for some reason or another. The "pony trainer" left to work for another barn shortly after I started working with her and took most of the other students with her when she left. I really liked the second trainer, but she unexpectedly left a few months after I started working with her. I was then assigned to the new "senior trainer" that had been hired. Her name was Kristine and she was a third generation horseperson who had just moved to the area. Due to her years of experience, the cost for Kristine to train me was higher than it was for the barn's new younger trainer. Because I really enjoyed working with her and my riding was improving each week, my mom willingly paid the higher fee.

My lesson had always been scheduled for Fridays at 7:00 pm, and each week my mom would rush home from work, hook up the trailer, load Ticky, get me in the car, and drive forty five minutes to the barn. When I first started working with Kristine, she told my mom she would rather not stay late for lessons on Fridays. When my mom explained that her work schedule at the time didn't allow for much flexibility on weeknights and weekends were pretty much out because of the barn's show day at the same time, she agreed to continue my lesson on the same schedule.

Everything was going well until one Friday night in December 2001. When we arrived for my lesson, Linda told us Kristine had gone home sick. Since we were already there, she suggested I do my lesson with the other trainer. My mom and I completely understood, so we agreed. It was very upsetting when the same thing happened several more times in the coming weeks. Each time there was a different excuse as to why Kristine wasn't there for my lesson. It's not that the other trainer wasn't nice; it's just that she wasn't my trainer, Kristine was. After the fourth incident, I refused to stay for my lesson. I was so upset I started crying on the way home and said I never wanted to go back.

CHAPTER 3

A Foal from Canada

Although I was very disappointed with the ongoing trainer situation at the barn, there were other things going on in my life at the time that made it more bearable. In the spring of 2001, Vicky told my mom she was thinking about adopting a PMU foal from Canada. Since my mom had no idea what a PMU foal was, Vicky explained how thousands of foals were born every year as the by-product of the female hormone replacement industry. While the mares were pregnant, their urine was collected and later processed by pharmaceutical companies. The result being that each year thousands of foals were in need of adoptive homes.

My mom did some research and found that many of the ranchers who bred these horses wanted their foals to go to good homes, so they bred quality registered horses, such as Quarter Horses and Paints, as well as, draft horses and draft cross sport horses. Wanting to do her part, my mom decided to adopt a draft cross foal from one of the adoption organizations out of Alberta, Canada. She thought we might get lucky and end up with a nice horse for me to show in the future, and if not, we would have a really big trail horse to ride. She sent in all our paperwork and the $1100 adoption fees with our request for a Thoroughbred/ Percheron cross colt. Soon afterward, we were advised that we met all of the adoption requirements and had officially been approved.

In April, the first foals started hitting the ground. The group we were working with would post photos and descriptions of the foals from each of the farms they worked with on their website so adopters could select the ones they wanted. Since we'd never owned or purchased a foal before, my mom explained what we were looking for and asked the woman who ran the group to pick one out for us. By July all of the foals had been born and the majority of them were already spoken for. Needless to say, we were getting a bit nervous at that point because no foal had been assigned to us.

The group's organizers posted a notice on their website looking for a farm to be the drop-off location for the sixteen Florida foals. It didn't take long for my mom to volunteer and tell them they could use our place. She was well aware we would have to make some changes to the areas where the foals would be held, including six foot high fencing, holding, sorting and loading areas, and a “buffer zone” to keep our horses well away from the quarantined foals. The transportation of the foals would begin in September, but since Florida was the farthest drop our load would be the last to go, sometime in November or December. That gave us plenty of time to prepare.

As the first groups of foals were being prepared for shipment, we were still waiting for one to be assigned to us. My mom contacted the group’s leader to check the status of our foal. She advised her that some of the other group members were going to a sale at a local farm that privately auctioned their foals every year. They’d picked up several Thoroughbred cross sporthorse prospects from them in the past that the adopters had been very pleased with. She assured my mom they would find the perfect foal for us there.

We were thrilled when we received an e-mail saying they had picked up our foal at the sale. Our foal, who we’d already decided to call Riley, was a black bay colt out of a Thoroughbred stallion who was a son of the great racehorse, Alydar, and a Percheron/Arab cross mare. Jennifer, one of the Canadian group members, had picked him out specifically for us. She e-mailed us personally to let us know he was a beautiful mover and the best looking foal in the group of sporthorse prospects. She said he was a “late” foal, having been born in early June, so he was somewhat smaller than the others. Not to worry though, she would keep an eye on him for us while he was at the holding farm. In the following months, she would periodically send us updates and pictures to let us know how Riley was doing.

In early December the Florida foals arrived at our house after their long trip from western Canada. The trailer pulled into our yard around dusk and as expected, the foals were all very tired, fuzzy, dirty, and some, including Riley, had nasty colds. It didn’t matter though; to everyone present they were all absolutely gorgeous! Although we had planned to keep the foals in the sorting/loading area until we figured out which ones were going home that night, Riley decided he didn’t want to be sorted and jumped a four foot gate into the holding area. Even at six months the boy had scope!

While Vicky, her husband, and the haulers loaded the foals leaving that night onto their new owner's trailers, our family, friends, neighbors, and other adopters had a chance to gawk at the new arrivals. There were small light horse foals, large draft foals that were already as big as Ticky, and every size in between. There were bays, blacks, chestnuts, and Paints; a veritable rainbow of colors. Once the last foal was loaded, the others were herded into the holding area to eat, drink and rest.

One of my jobs while the foals were at our house was to enforce our strict quarantine procedures. I had to make sure anyone who had been near the foals disinfected their hands and shoes before walking around our property. After all the foals left for their new homes, I helped my mom disinfect the foal areas and we kept our horses away from them for three months. All of our precautions worked very well because for the four years that we were the Florida drop, none of our horses ever picked up any type illness from the foals.

Vicky graciously offered to halter break Riley for us and keep him at her place for his three week quarantine. It worked out great for us because we had no experience working with foals, much less one that had been barely handled by humans. Since she had also adopted a foal, Riley had some equine companionship during his few weeks at Aunt Vicky's School of Horse Etiquette.

Once Riley finished prep school, we brought him home to meet his new pasture mates. Initially we were going to try to keep him in a separate paddock with Bo for a few weeks until Cheyenne, who could be extremely bossy in the pasture, got used to the idea of having him around. Being the intelligent equine he was, Bo had other plans. As soon as we put them in together, he took one look at Riley, walked over to the fence and jumped it from a stand-still so he could join Cheyenne in the pasture.

On to plan B; we weren't sure how Ticky would react to our new family member, but he was our only other option. Ticky seemed to immediately understand that he was Riley's "big brother" and was more than willing to stay with him. Riley loved having his own playmate and would tag along with Ticky everywhere he went. I have to admit, watching him grow and flourish in the months and years that followed was a truly incredible experience.

CHAPTER 4

The Hunter/Jumper Barn Saga Continues

After the arrival of Riley and our decision to leave the first hunter/jumper facility, my mom made arrangements for me to train at a barn that opened about five miles from our house. The trainer, Jen, was relatively young, very nice, and really tried to promote a family friendly atmosphere. When I worked with her she was always patient and kind, and made us feel welcome from the very start.

Most of the kids at the barn were friendly, with the exception of two older girls. The first one seemed to decide from the minute she met me that her purpose in life was to torture me. She was a year older than me and her family lived in a huge house on a lake in an affluent town nearby. She and her mom shared an old school horse they'd bought and they had been taking lessons with Jen for a couple of years. Because of that, she acted like the barn was her personal domain. Soon after I started trailering in for lessons, she began making nasty comments to the other girls about me when she knew I would overhear her in an attempt to stir up trouble. If I left my things in the tack stall at shows unattended, they would disappear, only to miraculously show up later when I no longer needed them.

At one show, she lost her back number and decided to take mine, write her number on the back, and use it for herself. When I went to get ready for my classes, my number was nowhere to be found. Of course, when my mom confronted her she played innocent saying she thought I was done showing; neither of us believed that one. Even more upsetting was that at the same show my new saddle pad vanished, never to be seen again. My mom was on to her and we both knew what had happened, but we couldn't prove it. It was so frustrating because the girl's parents would buy her the top of the line, most expensive saddle pads available and she had to take the $30 special my mom had bought me specifically for the show.

The girl also loved trying to make me feel inferior in an attempt to shake my confidence. After having her father buy a new GPA helmet from one of the tack shops at a show, she came back to the barn and literally shoved it in my face saying he had spent $400 for it. She then asked how much my helmet cost. If I was in a class with her or one of the other students from the barn, she would tell me things like, "You'll never beat me; I'm a better rider than you." Or, "She always wins those classes because she has a Warmblood. You and Ticky don't stand a chance."

Periodically, she'd leave me alone for a while to focus on other things. Yet just when I'd start to relax and think the tormenting was over, she'd come back at me full force. I suppose I should have been impressed by her, but I wasn't, and I guess that really annoyed her.

The other girl also lived in an exclusive upscale neighborhood on the other side of town. She was two years older than me and the biggest, most spoiled brat I had ever met in my life. Apparently, her horse was the most expensive one in the barn and she made sure everyone knew it. Like the other girl, she was fortunate that her parents could afford to buy her the best of everything and I couldn't understand why she felt the need to throw it in everyone else's face all the time.

Sometimes we'd go to shows that were attended by the kids from her previous barn and inevitably the girls would get together to devise some nasty plot against me. At a Fox Cry Farm show in September 2002 I was schooling Ticky in the ring when I noticed one of the girl's friends riding toward me. As she approached I said, "Outside," and hugged the rail. I couldn't believe it when, as she passed me, she purposely kicked me in the knee. Neither Ticky nor I were expecting it and the impact caused him to step sideways into the fence squashing my other leg against it. I couldn't believe someone would do that! Not surprisingly, I saw my two barn mates laughing outside the ring and the girl who kicked me smiling at them.

The funny thing was the mothers of those girls were always friendly and nice. I couldn't understand how they could be so sweet, while their daughters were so hateful. The other kids and parents made us feel welcome too, even though I wasn't at the barn all the time like some of them were. I really enjoyed being able to participate in weekly group lessons, trail rides throughout the property and summer camps with the other kids. All in all, I had a lot of fun while I was there.

Just prior to leaving Kristine, I had started competing in Short Stirrup. Rather than let me get more experience at that level, Jen kept raising the jumps until we were in the 2'3" – 2'6" range in just a few short months. She wanted me to be at the same height as the other kids around my age, but it was too much too fast. Ticky had always been a little strong and Kristine had been working with me on keeping a consistent quiet pace, but as the jumps got higher, we got faster. Rather than work on control, Jen suggested that Ticky and I do jumpers. I was excited by the prospect of doing what my idols did and felt I was ready to face the challenge. The problem was, her idea of coaching me in jumpers entailed yelling to me on course, "Gallop, slow down, turn, gallop, turn, slow down!" The adrenaline would be pumping as Ticky and I maneuvered around the ring like a whirlwind trying to go as fast as we could. My mom, on the other hand, would be holding her breath the entire time.

One of my most memorable events while working with Jen occurred in December 2002. Margie Engle hosted a riding clinic at the Grand Cypress Equestrian Center that Ticky and I were able to attend with some of the other barn kids. Having the opportunity to participate in a clinic with Margie was indescribable! I knew it was something many other young riders would have loved to do and I was extremely thankful I was able to be a part of it.

Margie was so patient and encouraging, I felt completely comfortable with her from the minute I entered the ring. We were in the group jumping 2' to 2'3" and Ticky was on his best behavior. At the end, she said I had done a really good job and told me she thought Ticky was very cute. I had my mom take a photo of Ticky and me with Margie after the clinic and asked her to sign a copy of her biography for me. I let her know I had read the book twice already and truly admired her dedication and determination. I told her I wanted to be just like her when I was older. She seemed very appreciative and thanked me for the comments. Margie was, and still is, an inspiration and role model for me.

It was around that time some issues had begun to surface that caused my mom to become concerned for my safety; Ticky had begun to refuse or run out at jumps without warning. We'd be headed for an obstacle, I'd think we were going, and he'd slam on the brakes or turn sharply to the side at the last minute. It was so exasperating because we knew he loved to jump and had always enjoyed going to shows. Everyone used to laugh when I'd do flat classes because I didn't have to ask Ticky to do anything. He'd hear the announcer say trot, canter, halt, etc. and just do it himself. It was great when I was first starting out because he knew what had to be done and took care of it for me.

As the months wore on, the situation got worse. Luckily I only came off once, at a show of course, but I ended up landing on my feet in front of a jump to the applause of the spectators. Jen seemed to have no idea how to fix the problems; her answer was to just keep going at the same level as if nothing was amiss. Finally, after one lesson during which Ticky absolutely refused to go over a particular jump, my mom decided she'd had enough and wasn't going to let the situation continue. She told me she was looking for another trainer.

In late January 2003, my mom found a more experienced trainer for me to work with who she hoped could solve the refusing issues. I have to say upfront that Marilyn's family, students and their families were overall the nicest and friendliest we'd ever been around. No one made us feel like outsiders and none of the kids were out to get each other. Unfortunately, since the barn was an hour away from us, I didn't have much time to hang around with them unless I was taking a lesson or we were at a show.

Our first schooling show with Marilyn went very well. She explained to me that in jumpers, it's not about going as fast as you can, but rather knowing where to cut out strides and how to pace your horse. Ticky and I were entered in some 2'6" jumper classes and placed high in each one. I was thrilled with the results and thought we were finally back on track.

Things continued to go well until just before the next show, which ended up being right after Ticky had his feet trimmed. I was very nervous because the jumper ring at the show facility was flooded, so management moved all the classes to a roped off grassy area near the barns. I don't know why, but I was afraid Ticky would jump the rope and run off with me; even though he'd never done anything remotely like that before. Between my anxiety and Ticky's uncooperativeness, we were disqualified from all our classes the first day because he kept refusing.

The next day Marilyn decided she would ride him in a couple of classes. When he'd refuse, she'd whack him with the riding crop until he went over the jump; I have to say, it got pretty ugly. She thought the problem might be with his feet, so she suggested we have someone look at him before I did any more showing or had another lesson.

After the show, my mom brought Ticky to the barn one morning to meet a man Marilyn said could figure out why he was refusing. The man said Ticky needed shoes, so since Marilyn's husband was a farrier, he put shoes on all four of his feet. While it did help a little, Ticky continued to be uncooperative over jumps.

A few weeks later, some of the barn kids were showing in Ocala at an "A" show. Because the showgrounds were about the same distance from our house as the barn, Marilyn suggested that we bring Ticky up there for our lesson. She decided we'd use one of the warm-up rings for our training. We started off well, but then Ticky refused a jump. When he refused it a second time, Marilyn started yelling at me, which only served to make the situation worse. The more she yelled at me, the more I mentally shut down. Finally when it seemed as though I couldn't do anything right, she said I had to get off Ticky because I was embarrassing her. She sent one of the other kids back to the barn to bring me her pony to ride. It was absolutely horrible.

My mom took her aside later and explained that I'm not used to having people yell at me and to please not do it again; but after that experience, I guess Marilyn somehow thought it was the way to get my attention. Once the yelling started, it didn't stop. I'm not sure if it was because I refused to cry in front of her, because she was frustrated with me, or maybe a little of both. Over time it got to the point that I would get physically sick and not want to practice at the showgrounds the day before a show started because I knew she'd yell at me in front of everyone.

One of the most humiliating episodes happened at one of the Fox Lea Farm summer camp shows. I was in the warm-up ring with Marilyn after a couple of disastrous 2' over fence classes in which I couldn't complete the courses. I had forgotten my crop and asked my mom to get it from the barn. While she was gone, Ticky started refusing again. In front of dozens of people, Marilyn screamed at me that if I couldn't ride my pony she wouldn't let me bring him to her barn. The only horses I would be allowed to ride would be school horses.

When my mom returned to the ring Marilyn told her I was done for the day. It wasn't until we got back to the barn that I started crying and told my mom what had happened. She asked if I wanted her to find a new trainer and I said, "No." It was so hard because we had so much fun with Marilyn and the people from the barn that I didn't want to leave them, yet when she was working with me it was a total nightmare. My mom ended up having another very long conversation with her that evening about not yelling at me. She tried again to explain to her that instead of making me work harder, yelling at me only made me shut down.

About a month later as we prepared for an upcoming show, Ticky refused a jump during my lesson and I went flying over his head. It was something that had never happened to me before and I was completely shocked. I knew I had to get back on him even though I was petrified. I just kept telling myself I couldn't give in and had to keep trying. Most importantly, I willed myself into not crying in front of Marilyn.

At the August North Florida Hunter Jumper "A" show I was entered in the Short Stirrup division, and although we didn't place in any classes the first day, Ticky behaved himself. As I was preparing in the warm-up ring the second day, he slammed on the brakes in front of a jump. I flipped over his head again, crashing into the jump poles on my back. It hurt so bad, I couldn't help crying. The gate person was holding the ring for me and my mom heard her tell the judge I'd probably scratch. I wasn't about to quit, so I got back on, took a warm-up jump, and went into the ring. I ended up getting a ribbon even though it wasn't my prettiest effort; I think maybe the judge gave me extra credit for at least getting back on.

CHAPTER 5

A New Horse and an Old Friend

When she heard I had come off of Ticky twice in one week, Vicky was absolutely livid and decided she was going to find a horse for me to free lease. Amazingly, within a week she found a lady who had a 16.2 hand bay Thoroughbred gelding that might work out for me. He was a former race horse that had been ridden by her 15-year-old daughter for a couple of years. She'd shown him successfully at local shows in the Children's Hunter divisions where he'd won various year-end awards. The girl had lost interest in riding, so for the last year he'd been used solely as her mother's trail horse. I knew from the moment I trotted him around his pasture and jumped a couple of cavalettis, Chance and I were meant to be together.

The only stipulation to his lease was that we had to pay for his mortality insurance. We dropped off a check the following weekend and loaded him on the trailer for the ride home. His owner had given my parents the option to buy him for $10,000 after six months if I really liked him. It was a wonderful offer, but we already had Ticky, Bo, Riley, and Cheyenne, and I knew it would be difficult for my parents to buy another horse for me. Once he was home though, I secretly dreaded the thought of having to someday give him back to his owner. I prayed every night that somehow we'd find a way to keep Chance.

I brought him out to Marilyn's farm for my lesson that first week and was extremely happy when she said she really liked him. Our first show together was the September 2003 Central Florida Hunter Jumper "A" show in Tampa. Since we'd only been together a couple of weeks, Marilyn entered me in the Short Stirrup division. I was absolutely thrilled when we won the Reserve Championship in the Short Stirrup Hunters!

Even though I had Chance to ride and show, I still wanted to ride Ticky too. Marilyn reluctantly agreed to do a second lesson each week with him, even though she'd pretty much written him off. My mom was determined not to give up on him and one morning she had a revelation; Ticky didn't want to jump because the shoes were bothering him. That same day, she and Vicky drove to our house during their lunch hour and pulled his shoes. When I brought him to Marilyn's for a lesson, he didn't refuse any jumps and she was amazed at the difference him. She seemed shocked when my mom told her she'd figured out he couldn't handle shoes.

One Saturday in October, as my mom and I were walking into the Home Depot near our house, my former trainer Kristine was walking out. We'd only seen her once since we'd left the barn she worked for almost two years earlier, and at the time, she had been living on the other side of Orlando. It took a few seconds for all of us to recognize each other, but once we did, we all started hugging. She asked if I still had Ticky and how he was doing. I filled her in on what had been going on and told her all about Chance. She said she had just moved to the area and we quickly figured out that her house was only about eight minutes away from ours. We talked for a little while and found out she was still working for Linda. Before she left, she gave my mom her card and told us to call her if she could help us with anything.

Even though Ticky had been doing much better without the shoes, I was a nervous wreck when we had our weekly lessons with Marilyn. I knew she didn't like him, which completely stressed me out. Knowing that, my mom asked me if I wanted her to call Kristine to see if she could help with the Ticky situation. When I had worked with her before she had been able to help me fix some issues with him, so maybe she could help me again. It would be a little strange having two trainers, but I was willing to try.

In just one lesson, Kristine was able to identify some of things I was doing that were helping to cause the refusals and run-outs. I was riding too far forward, I would sometimes shove Ticky at the jump, and would even "jump" forward out of the saddle as he lifted off the ground. We worked on my position and saw a huge difference almost immediately. Once those problems were solved, we had to break him of all the bad habits he'd learned. Kristine was definitely up for the challenge, which it meant I wouldn't have to bring him to Marilyn's barn ever again.

After a few weeks, Kristine joined my mom and me at a local show to coach me and see how Ticky would do. We pinned in the top three in each of our classes, some of which had over ten riders in them. But most importantly, I had a great time showing my pony. I was very relaxed the entire day and really enjoyed hanging out with just my mom and Kristine. When my mom mentioned something to her about attending other shows in the future, she said really didn't like going to shows and there was no reason why we needed to have a trainer with us anyway. Since my mom had been to every show I'd ever attended and helped me whenever I practiced at home, Kristine felt she could easily coach me at shows. I thought it was a great idea, even though my mom wasn't completely convinced.

We also talked to Kristine about me continuing to ride Chance with Marilyn. Outside of the ring, I loved hanging out with her and I really liked all the people at her barn. My mom felt the same way and neither one of us wanted to break away from them. On the other hand, I loved working with Kristine and always felt extremely comfortable around her. If I didn't understand something she was trying to teach me, she would find a different way to explain it or show me how to do it, rather than yell at me like Marilyn. Plus, she came to our house for lessons, which made things really easy for my mom.

In November, I brought Chance and Ticky to a local show with Marilyn. As we were getting ready to leave on Friday afternoon, Ticky got hung up in his lead rope which caused a deep rope burn on the back of one of his rear pasterns. All I could really do to help him was hose the injury off, clean it up and put some antibiotic cream on it. He wasn't lame, so we decided to take him with us to the show, realizing we still might have to scratch. I was quite surprised when he schooled well that same evening and never took a bad step. Saturday he was moving nicely, but near the end of his first course he ran out. Marilyn was standing at the gate with my mom, and when he ducked out she threw up her hands and said to her, "Why do you even bother bringing him."

My mom said she turned to her and said emphatically, "Because Alyx wants to."

What Marilyn didn't realize was that Ticky and I had been very successful since Kristine began working with us. I knew the only reason he'd run out was because his leg must have started to bother him. I was very proud of my pony for at least trying. That day I made the decision to never take him to a show with Marilyn again. I wasn't going to let her put him down in front of everyone or shake my confidence any more.

On Christmas Eve, my mom decided to do something very unusual; rather than put my gifts under the tree so I could open them with everyone else, she presented me with a scroll that read:

Dear Alyx,
It's Christmas Eve; a time for family, food and fun,
And as always you'll receive presents when all is said and done.
But it won't be as easy as it's been in the past,
You'll have to find them this time; let's see if you last.
You must follow directions and listen to clues,
In order to receive what is your due.
Don't try to rush and get in a hurry,
Or you may miss a gift amid all the flurry.
Your instructions must be found before you can look,
I promise none will be as long as a book.
Once you have found them, bring them back here,
Read them aloud and be sure to be clear.
Now go to the drawer and look deep inside,
That's where your first clue decided to hide.
Ah, but what drawer can it be, you may ask,
Find it and you'll have completed your first task.

I quickly found the clue in the dining room buffet which lead me to my first few gifts and the next clue. Each new poem sent me from one end of the house to the other as I searched for the hidden stashes of presents. Finally, I found the fourth and final clue:

Here's your last clue so be sure to think clearly,
It's something you'll love both deeply and dearly.
I wanted to put it under the tree and lights,
Oh, but wouldn't that have been such a sight!
The gift is quite special, and one of a kind,
This is something I know you surely will find.
You must promise to love it forevermore,
Now walk into the foyer and open the front door.

It seemed kind of odd that she would tell me to walk out the front door for a gift, but I was quite intrigued and went along with it. As I stepped through the doorway into the cold evening air, I saw my dad standing in the yard, illuminated by the porch lights, holding Chance by his lead rope. I thought Chance looked very cute with the giant red bow attached to his blanket and the Santa cap on his head. My dad just stood there smiling at me and it took a couple of moments for me to realize that Chance was my Christmas present; he was now officially my horse! I couldn't believe it! All our family and friends were crying. I just kept thanking my mom and dad over and over while I hugged Chance around the neck. He was the most wonderful Christmas present I'd ever received!

In mid-January we took Chance to a schooling show with Marilyn and her students. I was placing very well in some large hunter and equitation classes and was feeling great. During one flat class my mom was standing with Marilyn and some of the other parents near the in-gate. When her other students would go by, she would remind them get their heels down or quietly offer some advice that they would be able to hear.

As I went by, she yelled loudly at me for something I can't even remember. She then laughingly turned to my mom and said in front of the other parents, "Don't you get sick of me yelling at your kid?"

My mom said she just looked her straight in the eye and said firmly, "As a matter of fact, I do."

She then turned back to the ring to watch me while they all stared at her in shock. I ended up placing second in that class, higher than any of Manilyn's other students. That same afternoon, I also won Reserve Champion honors in the Children's Equitation 13 & Under.

A couple of weeks later Ticky and I went to our first show with my "trainer mom." It was the first of a series put on by the Florida Hunter Classic Association called Horseshows in the Park and it was held at Wickham Park in Melbourne. My mom chose that particular show because she knew it was one Marilyn didn't attend. I was excited at the prospect of showing in a couple of hunter and jumper classes, but I could tell my mom was very nervous, even though she tried not to let it show. Vicky was kind enough to come with us as moral support for my mom. I was so glad she did because she definitely helped keep us both calm.

My first class was a Novice Jumper class and there were eleven riders in it. Kristine had told me to ride the jumper class like an equitation class; keep control, don't rush. There was one jump that had freaked me out while we were schooling, and in our first class I rushed Ticky to it, causing him to duck out. I knew it was my fault when it happened, so I calmly took him to it a second time without issue, and we were able to finish the course with four jumping faults and two time faults. The first class was definitely the worst for both my mom and me, but we had gotten through it unscathed and were ready to move on.

There were ten riders in my second Novice Jumper class, which was run as a power and speed. I kept telling myself, control, control, control. At one point in the course, we had to do a really tight rollback. Everyone was going into it fast, which meant their horses needed more room to turn. Knowing Ticky was small and agile; I got over the first jump of the rollback, took him down to a trot for a couple of steps to turn and got to the second jump in two strides. Throughout the course I was also able to make other tight turns and jump at sharper angles than the larger horses. None of the other riders were able to beat my time and we ended up winning the class! That afternoon we also did well in our hunter classes, which had about the same number of riders as the jumper classes. The best thing was my mom and I had survived, and it was probably the most fun I'd ever had at a show!

We decided to attend the FHCA February show, and since Marilyn was going to be at HITS that weekend, we took both Ticky and Chance. I placed well with both horses in every class we were entered in; but the highlights for me were winning the power and speed class again with Ticky and winning the Junior Equitation Over Fences Challenge with Chance. I found out after the show that I would be receiving the 2004 FHCA Winter Series High Point Child Rider award at their upcoming April show. I was having a great time and my hard work was paying off; that was the way it was supposed to be!

It was after that show my mom and I made the decision that Kristine would be my riding instructor for both Ticky and Chance. With newfound confidence, my mom agreed to be my coach when I practiced at home and showed. I didn't realize at the time that it would be the beginning of what would be a wonderful opportunity for us to spend lots of time together doing something we both loved.

CHAPTER 6

Something You Can Never Prepare For

In the months that followed, Chance proved to be a wonderful teacher who knew his job and always took charge of the situation if I was hesitant. We spent most of 2004 going to various local shows and were quite successful in the hunter and equitation classes, winning a number of grand and reserve championships. One show I will always remember was held at a New Smyrna Beach farm in June. By that time, Kristine had left Linda's barn and was working with a small group of her own students. She had decided to join us at the show and brought some of them with her. I really enjoyed hanging out with everyone in between our classes and cheering the other kids on when they showed.

Earlier in the day, Ticky and I had won the Grand Championship in the Pony Hunters, and Chance and I had won Grands in the Children's Hunter and Open Equitation divisions. The final class was our medal class, and I ended up being the very last rider of the day. The other competitors in the class were older teenagers; including one of Kristine's other students. From the moment we entered the ring, it was as if Chance and I knew exactly what the other was thinking. Everything just seemed to flow and we completed every test that was asked of us perfectly. As soon as we finished our course, everyone around the ring, including the show staff, judge and other riders were applauding us. As we approached the gate to leave the ring, the farm's owner yelled out, "The last ride of the day was the best ride of the day. Great job 267!" That brought another round of applause from the spectators. Needless to say, we won the class and I was beside myself with happiness!

Riding the big circuits all the time was definitely not an option for me, but I had hoped to enter a few "A" rated shows during the upcoming 2005 season. To get me past the first time jitters, my mom decided to take me to a couple of "C" rated shows being held at Fox Lea Farm in October and November. We ended up doing pretty well at both and I was looking forward to trying some bigger shows in the coming months.

Unfortunately, everything came to an abrupt halt one sunny November afternoon a week after the second show. My dad had met me at the end of the road and told me the vet was at our house because Chance had colicked. I will never forget the scene that unfolded before me as I quickly walked home from the bus stop. As I approached our house, I saw Donna's truck in our driveway. Just past it, I could see her standing with my mom next to Chance, who was laying down on his side in the front yard. When I reached them, my mom explained that he hadn't been feeling well for several hours. Donna had given him some medication and he seemed to be more comfortable; they thought the worst was over.

Since Donna had to leave for another call, she helped us lead Chance into the backyard so we could continue to watch him. She was concerned that he wouldn't eat or drink, so she said she'd stop by again to check on him in a couple of hours on her way home. She told us it would be best to just let him keep resting until then. If he started to show signs of distress though, she wanted us to call her immediately.

When she returned as promised two hours later Chance was still resting on his side, but within a half hour his condition began to spiral downward literally before our eyes. Donna checked his vitals and based on his deteriorating condition, told us the only option was to immediately take him to the large animal hospital at the University of Florida. She made all the necessary calls for us while we prepared for our trip.

When we arrived at the hospital the medical team met us in the parking lot and rushed Chance into the clinic. He looked absolutely miserable and his gums had turned blue; it was devastating for us to watch. They attempted to improve Chance's condition with more medication, eventually moving him from the examination area into a stall. After several hours passed without success, the surgeon determined that the only alternative was emergency surgery. He believed the colic was the result of an impaction and said Chance would probably be ready to go home in a week. By then it was after midnight. Since there was nothing more we could do before the procedure, the surgeon suggested we go home. I hugged and kissed Chance goodbye, and told him I loved him. I was very upset that I had to leave him knowing he was so sick, but I knew he would have the best care available.

Sadly, we found out the next morning that it wasn't an impaction as they had originally thought, but a severe twist in his intestine that turned out to be much worse than anyone could have anticipated. Apparently when horses have a twist they are in so much pain they tend to throw themselves around and flail, so it's relatively apparent what the problem is. Chance had not behaved that way at all; he had actually been quite stoic from the time my parents had first noticed him acting strangely and removed him from the pasture. Although the surgeon did everything within his power to help Chance, his internal organs sustained significant damage resulting in the removal nearly three quarters of his small intestine. On top of that, many of his vital systems had been severely compromised. His prognosis after the surgery was uncertain at best.

Donna followed up with the surgeon throughout the entire episode for us. She was able to give us the layman's version of what was going on with Chance. Knowing that we might have to make the decision to put him down, my mom, Donna and I had several long discussions about what his quality of life would be if he was able to recover. As I attempted to process everything that was happening, Donna suggested that my mom and I go up to visit him and see for ourselves how he looked. She was confident that we would know what to do when we saw him.

Two days after his surgery, my mom and I headed up to Gainesville to visit Chance. Although we all prayed and held out every last hope for his recovery, the dreaded phone call came as were driving through Ocala. The surgeon told my mom he had taken a turn for the worse overnight; it was time to make the decision we had all wished to avoid. I heard my mom ask him what he thought and saw her face go white at his response. She told me later that he had said if Chance was his horse, he would put him down. As we both choked back tears, she told him to go ahead with the procedure. On Saturday morning, November 13, 2004, Chance was humanely euthanized.

In the ten years my family had owned horses, we'd never had to deal with a catastrophic illness before. Thankfully Donna was there to help us through that difficult situation; something we sincerely appreciated. She was truly a voice of reason and understanding amid all the chaos. For that, I will always be extremely grateful. Within a few days, we found out that quite a number people we knew had heard about Chance's illness from Vicky and had been keeping us in their prayers, including his former owner. I was amazed at how many people sent us their condolences because they truly cared about Chance and me.

I was totally devastated by the loss; I'd lost my teacher, my partner and my friend. I completely shut down because of my grief and told everyone I didn't want to ride any more. A month passed; I refused to ride and barely spent any time in the barn. Friends and acquaintances contacted my mom offering to let me ride their horses, but I wasn't interested. As the Christmas holidays approached, Kristine and my mom decided it was time to try to get me back in the saddle. Finally, after a lot of persuasion and cajoling, they convinced me that it wasn't fair to ignore Ticky because of what had happened. Reluctantly I agreed to begin schooling him and take lessons again. It wasn't easy for me, but I knew giving up riding would have been disrespectful to Chance's memory after everything he'd taught me.

Fortunately my mom had decided to insure Chance when she bought him. It ended up covering most of the cost of his medical expenses and provided us with money to buy another horse. In January, the life insurance check arrived and my mom cautiously suggested we might want to start looking for a new horse. Although I loved my pony and was very comfortable with him, we all had known for some time that I had grown too tall for him. While I wasn't thrilled about looking for a new partner, because no horse could replace Chance or be the incredible teacher he had been, I halfheartedly agreed to go horse shopping with my mom and Kristine.

CHAPTER 7

Destiny and the Green Thoroughbred

In no time, leads on potential horses came flooding in and the screening process began. Finally, having narrowed down a few choices, my mom, Kristine and I drove to Ocala to meet some possible partners. After several disappointing prospects, Kristine suggested we check out a horse she had found in an ad that morning. Although she never looked for horses on the Internet, something compelled her to look in the Ocala classifieds before she left her house. She had been drawn immediately to an ad for a nine-year-old16.3 hand chestnut Thoroughbred gelding. From his picture, he was quite a good-looking horse, but we would definitely have to check him out to see if he was what we were looking for. Kristine called the owner, got directions to her house, and we were on our way to her farm on the other side of town.

As my mom followed the directions she was given, we passed a sign stating we were entering Summerfield. She immediately commented that we had purchased Ticky five years earlier from a woman in Summerfield and it was the only other time we'd even been in the area. Shortly thereafter we passed a side road that she thought might have been the one we had taken when we bought Ticky; what a coincidence that the horse we were going to look at lived in the same town! A few minutes later and a few miles further down the main road we found our turn.

The road, if it could even be called that, was actually two bare ruts through grass. We bounced along for several hundred yards when my mom said she was beginning to feel a sense of déjà vu. The three of us were looking for the woman's house number when my mom noticed a green sign in front of a house down the road on the right. She told Kristine if the sign ahead of us said Forest Hill Farm, that's where we got Ticky. How weird would that be? Sure enough as we got closer, she saw that it was the same sign she had remembered. I felt a little chill go down my spine as my mom started mimicking the Twilight Zone theme song. Directly across the street was the home we were looking for; it also happened to be the one where the red roan pony had been. It was starting to get really weird.

Upon our arrival Dawn, the owner, brought us out back to see a lovely well-built Thoroughbred with a large cross-shaped blaze on his face. She introduced him as "JC" or "Jay", telling us he responded to both. She said he had never raced and had been with her family most of his life. There had been no doubt when you looked at Chance that he was a Thoroughbred; Jay, on the other hand, looked more like a Warmblood or even an Appendix with his stockier build. Kristine's first impression of him was that he had a kind eye.

I held my breath as Dawn walked him over to meet me. As I extended my hand to pet his nose, he promptly licked it. For me, and I think Jay too, it was love at first sight. While we stood there talking, he sniffed and nuzzled me as I continued to pet him. I knew I probably should look at more horses, but I silently prayed that he would work out.

Kristine asked Dawn to ride him around a bit before I got on to try him. Although he was a bit rusty, he had a very good foundation. Once I had done some flatwork with him, Dawn suggested we go across the street so I could take him over a few jumps. As we walked over to the neighbor's house, my mom told her how we had purchased a pony from that same neighbor several years before. She laughed when my mom did her Twilight Zone theme song impression again. It was very disconcerting when she proceeded to bring us to the exact same pasture where I had tried Ticky. When I entered the gate, I heard my mom tell Kristine that she was really getting freaked out by the situation. She said it had to be some kind of sign; there was no way everything that had happened so far that day could just be a series of coincidences!

After I took Jay over some jumps, Kristine called me over to ask what I thought. My mom told me later it was quite apparent to her what my response would be based on my huge smile. She was very concerned though because she knew getting Jay to the show ring would not be an easy task even though he knew the basics. He had never been to a horse show in his life; in fact, he hadn't been taken off the property in the six or so years Dawn had owned him, except when her daughter had ridden him around the neighborhood. In addition, he hadn't been ridden for nearly a year, so he lacked any type of muscle tone. Yet, as Kristine had suggested, we had to look past all that and see his potential.

Turning him into a show horse would require a huge commitment on my part, but I inherently knew whatever I learned on my journey with

Jay would benefit me for the rest of my life. I understood completely that I would be responsible for training him; Kristine, Vicky and my mom would be there to guide me along the way, but I would have to put in a lot time and do virtually all of the work in the saddle myself. People always told me I had an incredible work ethic for someone my age and this undertaking would definitely put that to the test. I must admit I felt a tinge of trepidation about the upcoming endeavor, but I sincerely believed I was ready to meet any challenges that would come my way.

My mom always said, "Everything happens for a reason; whether you think it's good or bad at the time. Eventually you'll understand why it happened because things always have a way of working out for the best."

I had to believe we didn't just find Jay by accident; we were meant to be partners. My mom, on the other hand, was extremely apprehensive. I had gotten to the point where I loved the excitement of the jumper ring and the technical aspects of equitation. Her goal had been to find a horse with experience as either a jumper or equitation horse, preferably both. We certainly didn't have to have a horse with experience at the big shows; a "made" horse like Chance with local experience would have been ideal. An essentially green horse with no show experience had not even been an option when we set out on our venture, but Kristine assured my mom that I could handle it. Seeing as I had my heart set on trying him out, she grudgingly agreed. She said I would have to make absolutely sure I wanted him when the time came to make the final decision as he would probably be the last horse she'd be able to buy for me.

Kristine and Dawn agreed on a sale price of $10,000 inclusive of Kristine's commission, and we made arrangements that day to take Jay home on a trial basis the following weekend. Once we got him home we had to keep him separate from our other horses until we decided if we were going to keep him or not. We had no idea at the time what a gregarious horse Jay was; an attention hog that loved any type of company, whether it was human, equine, or even canine. While he was not happy about being unable to socialize with the boys, he made the best of it. At least he seemed to enjoy seeing me every day. Once he passed his vet check, I became the proud owner of a new horse whose show name became *Alchemist's Gold.*

After two weeks of training boot camp working on the flat and over fences, it was time to take Jay to his very first horse show. We chose a local 4-H show that was being held at Clarcona Horseman's Park in Apopka and entered him in three under saddle classes. On January 22, 2005, Jay stepped off the trailer at showgrounds, looked at the chaos around him, and literally froze every muscle in his body. He seemed to be utterly shocked by the sights and commotion. His eyes were so wide they looked like they were going to pop out of his head. I think if he could have grabbed me and wrapped his legs around my body for security, he would have. I was able to lead him to his stall without incident, but as I unhooked the lead rope I could see he was trembling. It was going to be a long day.

Kristine wanted me to get Jay used to the surroundings, so she told me to meet her in the schooling ring by the main hunter arena. Riding from the barns to the ring was quite a challenge as he was completely overwhelmed by the entire situation and insisted on taking stiff little baby steps through the throng of horses and people. My mom walked next to us the entire time, worried that I would experience some mishap along the way. I knew she wanted to be ready to grab either Jay's reins or me if the situation arose. As we approached the ring, a girl of about eight or nine burst from the crowd and ran straight for us. By Jay's reaction you would have thought she was some kind of horse-eating monster. I really thought he was going to have a meltdown or something, so I immediately braced myself in the saddle in preparation for an explosion. Thankfully, she turned before getting too close and ran off in another direction.

Little did I realize that schooling in the warm-up ring would be a completely daunting experience. Even though the ring was huge and there weren't many riders schooling, Jay was awestruck by all the activity as horses passed by us in a multitude of directions and people milled around the perimeter. I was very intimidated by Jay's size and strength as he reacted to his surroundings, but I knew for us to succeed I had to conquer my fear and work through the situation with him. After literally dozens of spooks and overly dramatic responses to anything and everything, Jay finally settled down enough for us to do some effective flatwork. It was completely nerve-wracking, but we got the job done.

The walk back to the barn was relatively uneventful and I began to think it wasn't going to be too bad after all.

As I anxiously awaited my first class, I began to express my concerns about how Jay might behave in the ring. My mom reminded me that no matter what happened, safety was the top priority. If Jay behaved in a manner that could result in injury to me or the other riders in the ring, I could excuse myself from the class. Her only advice to me was, "Do the best you can with what you've got." It was a phrase I would become very familiar with over the next couple of years.

Shortly thereafter, with Kristine, my mom and my dad watching, Jay was on his best behavior and we pinned fifth out of twenty in our first Hunter Under Saddle class. Unfortunately, all the excitement seemed to overcome him during our second under saddle class. When the announcer asked us to trot, Jay decided to finally have his meltdown. As I was trying to circle in the middle of the ring to give us more room, he stopped dead in his tracks refusing to move forward. Then he started rocking forward and backward in place, oblivious to my commands, getting higher and higher off the ground each time. When I was finally able to re-engage his brain and regain forward momentum, he decided he couldn't move in a straight line and began side passing across the ring. I have to say, his form was beautiful, but it definitely wasn't what I was asking for. I was completely frustrated, nervous and embarrassed thinking everyone was watching our unusual display. At some point during our little exhibition, I vaguely remember hearing Kristine's voice from outside the ring telling me to get him between my hands and legs and push him forward. I focused on those words, eventually recapturing his attention and getting him under control.

To my utter relief, we had a little break before our final class and I was able to pull myself together and mentally re-group. I was thrilled when we finished second out of fourteen in our Hunt Seat Equitation on the Flat class. All things considered, not too bad a showing for our first time out.

The following weekend we brought Jay to a schooling show at Sumter Equestrian Center in Bushnell for some over fence classes. We made sure we arrived in plenty of time to school in the ring before the classes started. As soon as he saw the judges stand on the side of the ring, Jay decided it was his mortal enemy and did everything in his power to remain as far away from it as possible. I must have taken him past it thirty times in both directions before we had to clear the ring, yet he still seemed to think it was going to viciously attack him whenever he got near it.

Our first two classes were a flat and an over fence in the Modified Child/Adult Equitation division at 2'3". We didn't place in either class because Jay's hysterics every time we passed the judge's stand were pretty impressive. In addition, he panicked at an unusually painted jump during our first course and ran out on it. While we waited for my next division to begin, I hoped I could finish the day without falling off. Fortunately, our Beginner Hunter classes at the same height went much better. We ended up pinning in both of our over fence and the under saddle classes without any more drama from Jay. I had to keep reminding myself that it was a whole new world for him and he had never been exposed to these things before. Sooner or later he would realize that nothing in the show ring was going to hurt him. I fervently hoped that someday he would get to a point where he actually enjoyed going to shows. Only time would tell.

After seeing Jay's apprehension at some of the show jumps, my mom came up with a great idea; she would build walls and gates for us to jump at home that would be unlike anything he'd ever see at a show in an attempt to desensitize him. If we could make him more comfortable jumping unusual obstacles in his own environment, the ones he'd see at horse shows would be no problem. Several years earlier, my mom and Vicky had built numerous pairs of basic standards for me so I could practice jumping in our arena at home. They'd worked perfectly for Ticky and Chance, but for Jay my mom was going to have to get a lot more creative.

She set out on her mission and in no time her first jump projects were complete. They were two free standing gates that were 2'6" high; one was a plank three board fence and the other a lattice fence, both painted white. To add some color and flamboyance, she attached artificial flower garlands to the planks and small floral bouquets to the lattice. Her next creations were two walls; one 18" high and the other 2'9" high. The smaller wall had a red brick design on one side and angled green, yellow and orange stripes on the other. On the larger wall she painted a faux grey and beige stone wall with a giant green lizard across it on one side. On the other side she painted two black arches on a white background with black dolphin silhouettes jumping over them. Even with my limited experience with Jay, I didn't try to fool myself into thinking he'd go over either wall easily.

During my first lesson with the new jumps he was very cooperative going over the smaller one on the brick side. Thinking I'd have better luck with the lizard than the dolphins, I asked my mom to face that side forward when she was setting up my course. As it turned out, it was not the best decision in that instance.

Kristine decided to wait until we were nearing the end of our lesson before she asked us to attempt the lizard jump. I was feeling very self-assured, especially since the smaller wall had been a non-issue for him. As we approached the jump I actually thought Jay was going to go, but at the last second he looked at the lizard and changed his mind. He slammed on the brakes so hard and fast, I was caught completely unaware and got dumped. I knew at that moment it was going to get ugly. I gingerly dusted the dirt off myself, got back on, and started my approach the second time; I was going to be ready for anything. I was thrilled when he took it, but he banged his front legs hard on the top of the wall going over. The next time he must have been expecting pain and ducked out quickly to the right at the last minute, dumping me again. I sat on the ground in disbelief, refusing to cry even though I had hit the ground so hard the breath had been knocked out of me. I took a couple of minutes to compose myself, then climbed back on and attempted the jump again. He slammed on the brakes a couple more times, but I was able to stay on. At that point I thought I was ready for anything. The next time he hit the breaks though, he decided to half rear and run to the left, dumping me a humiliating third time.

Sitting on the ground covered in dirt and engulfed in a cloud of dust, I glanced over to where Jay had run into the corner of the arena and noticed our neighbor standing by the fence watching the proceedings. It was bad enough Kristine and my mom had witnessed the debacle; it had just become a public display. I could feel tears begin to well up in my eyes. In the over five years I'd had Ticky, I'd only come off him three times and I'd never come off Chance at all. With Jay I'd already been dumped three times in a matter of minutes. I prayed it wasn't a foreshadowing of what the future would hold for me; I didn't think my butt could handle much more.

No matter what, I was not going to feel sorry for myself. Jay was going to go over that wall like a gentleman, even if I had to spend the rest of the night getting him to do it. I dusted myself off for what I expected was the last time, wiped my eyes and waited for Kristine to bring Jay back to me. Without a word she gave me a leg up. My mom handed me my riding crop, and thus armed, I set out for the jump. Two strides out I could feel him start to pull back so I squeezed him with my legs and popped him on the butt with the crop. I think the shock of the crop was just the encouragement he needed. It wasn't a pretty jump by any standard, but he got over it. We took it again a few more times until he eventually stopped resisting and Kristine said we were done.

I could tell my mom was really stressed out by what had just transpired. Jay was a big boy and obviously more quick and agile on his feet than we had anticipated. Her main concern whenever we rode horses was always safety; I knew she was having major doubts about Jay at that moment. No one said much as we made our way to the barn. In an attempt to lighten everyone's mood as I untacked my horse, she affectionately renamed the lizard jump the "*Wall of Pain*." I couldn't help but laugh as she started singing some ridiculous lyrics about it to the tune of The Police's song "*King of Pain*." I never could have imagined how sore I would be after that lesson; the wall had definitely earned its new name.

In time, our collection of jump obstacles grew to include some very unique and potentially terrifying creations built specifically for Jay. We needed to practice over skinny jumps, so my mom built a six foot wide bright yellow lattice gate which Jay surprisingly had no issues with. Then she decided to build 3' high 3' wide free standing wall that she could put under a six foot rail. On one side of the skinny wall she painted the Japanese symbol for good fortune on a bright orange and yellow background. The other side was a white background covered in red, yellow, orange, blue, and green spots of varying sizes. It looked like a rainbow of bubbles and was not one of Jay's favorites. Another fun one was a free standing eight foot wide wood frame about 2'6" high with artificial palm fronds attached to it that looked like some bizarre hedge.

One of my mom's personal favorites was a brightly colored wooden sunburst attached to a rail that could be set in jump cups.

I have to admit, her final two motifs were my favorites. Since the *Wall of Pain* was too heavy for one person to easily maneuver, my mom decided to remove both of the painted plywood sides from the frame. She was able to turn them into much lighter individual walls by attaching legs on each end with a footer attached for support. That left her with two blank sides for more artistic scenes. Rather than leave the painted arches on the dolphin wall, she cut them out completely so the bottom was open and then cut the top so it looked like waves. On the opposite side she painted a grey stone wall around the arches. Above the wall the head, hands and wings of a white horned monster reminiscent of those found in the book, *Where the Wild Things Are,* could be seen peeking over the top. Much to everyone's surprise, that one didn't bother Jay too much.

The new design opposite the lizard was a totally different story. I really wanted a Chinese dragon jump and asked my mom if she would paint one for me. That one wall ended up taking twice as long as any of the others, but it turned out to be absolutely amazing! On a black background she painted a beautifully detailed white dragon with orange and red flames on his back, legs and tail. In the upper left corner painted in bright orange were the Japanese symbols for "champion," and in the bottom left the symbols for "horseman." I had to spend quite a long time convincing Jay the dragon wasn't going to eat him.

Even Riley, who doesn't get flustered by any jump, had to do a double take the first time I took him over it. As we approached the wall, he dropped his head nearly to the ground to get a better look at it. He went over without a problem, but my mom said the look on his face was utterly hysterical! I can pretty much guarantee that neither Jay nor Riley will ever see any jumps at a horse show as "scary" as they ones we have at home.

CHAPTER 8

The Rated Show Roller Coaster

During our first few months together, my mom and I took Jay to as many different venues as possible to expose him to different environments. It didn't take long for me to come to realization that I was the "experienced" half of our partnership and it was up to me to help Jay do his best. Ticky and Chance both had extensive show records and had been able to help and teach me along the way; riding, training, and showing an essentially green horse was a totally new experience.

When we had initially looked at Jay, Dawn told me that he was very sensitive and reacted to his rider's emotions. If I was nervous, he would be nervous. If I was confident, he would be surer of himself. It was very strange at first, but over time it taught me to focus on what I was doing and the task at hand when riding. If I made a mistake, I had to let it go and not worry about it. Similarly, if there was something going on around me, I learned I had to ignore it and not let it affect me. Of course, there were always those moments from time to time, especially in the beginning, when I would let a situation get the better of me. In those instances Jay would have to mentally fend for himself, which was usually not a good thing.

It soon became apparent that Jay was undergoing an amazing transformation as a result of all the time and effort I was putting in. His body had gone from virtually no muscle tone to extremely defined and well developed. His fear of horse-eating judge's stands, menacing photographers, and other nonexistent monsters was eventually overcome. He generally placed quite well and even won numerous championships in hunters and equitation at local shows, which soon had me eager to try something more challenging.

In April, with Kristine's blessing, my mom and I set out for Fox Lea Farm's "C" rated show. Right after we arrived, I ran into one of Marilyn's students and found out she would be showing in some of the same classes. When my mom and I eventually ran into Marilyn, we were all very polite and friendly. She seemed very surprised that we were at the show without Kristine and that my mom would be coaching me, especially since she would never even let me warm up at the shows unless she was in the ring.

After schooling Jay, one of the girls from Marilyn's barn approached me as I gave him a bath and asked all kinds of questions about him. I suppose she was sent over to get info so they could figure out if they knew him. I wasn't about to tell her that he'd spent six years as a virtual pasture ornament; they could just keep guessing.

Much to my delight, we won Reserve Grand Champion honors in the Children's Hunter division and received top placings in several medal classes that weekend. Most importantly, we had successfully conquered our first rated show and I felt invincible!

Unfortunately, the following weekend didn't go quite as well. We had decided to attend a series of four RMI shows held at HITS Post Time Farm in Ocala. For the first one, my mom and I planned to go up on Friday so I would have a chance to school Jay and familiarize him with the surroundings. Since it was an "A" show, Kristine had agreed to come up for the day on Sunday. I think my mom and I were both rather intimidated knowing all the "big name" trainers in the Central Florida area would be in attendance and we would probably stand out like sore thumbs.

We arrived around noon to ensure I would have plenty of time to school in the show ring before they closed it. Jay was a little goofy at first as he walked around the barns, spooking at just about anything that moved. Since my Children's Hunter classes would be held in the pony ring on the far end of the showgrounds, we gingerly made our way over to it through the barn and vendor areas. When we arrived, there were dozens of kids already schooling or waiting around the in-gate for their turn to go in. Not knowing how Jay would react, I was extremely nervous when I finally got my chance to go in. I knew my position was horribly stiff, but I couldn't help myself. It was a huge relief to get out of the ring when we finally finished going over each of the jumps.

That night and Saturday morning it rained profusely, so the grounds were a giant mud bog. The Children's division was at the end of the day, and because of the weather, things were moving very slowly in the pony ring. About mid-afternoon the show management decided to move my classes to the main hunter ring since the classes scheduled there were almost done. As we made our way over to the ring to warm-up, my heart was pounding and I was having second thoughts about wanting to show.

Jay was actually quite cooperative as I schooled him, but the muddy footing made me quite anxious. I was afraid Jay was going to slip in the mud and fall, so I started to panic. The strange thing was he hadn't taken even one bad step while I warmed him up, having been very surefooted over all the practice jumps. As I waited for my turn to go into the ring, my apprehension continued to grow. Realizing what was happening, my mom told me I wasn't there to win ribbons; I was there for the experience and to see how Jay would handle the situation.

Not surprisingly, I was so nervous I stiff-armed Jay all the way around the course. He did slip a little in one of the corners during my warm-up, but it was barely noticeable. I wished that had been our only mistake of the day; it was nothing compared to what happened during my two hunter rounds. I missed half the lead changes and threw myself forward in the saddle as we went over the jumps, which in turn, threw Jay off balance. I could only imagine how hideous it must have looked. I was sure everyone was thinking I was a backyard rider with a backyard horse that didn't belong there.

To make matters even worse, I was totally humiliated and embarrassed when I was ridiculed by a well known trainer from the Central Florida area who was standing at the in-gate as I exited the ring after my second round. He was with the mother of one of his students on the opposite side of the gate from my mom. As Jay and I approached them, he looked directly at us and said sarcastically and loudly to the woman, "Aren't you glad you don't have that," obviously referring to Jay.

She agreed and they both laughed at us as we walked out. I was ready to burst into tears, but refused to cry in front of them.

My mom looked right at him after I passed and said loudly to me, "Aren't you glad that's not your trainer."

I was too upset to see what his reaction was.

As we made our way back to the barn, my mom tried to do what she could to comfort me. When I hopped off Jay next to his stall, she hugged me and told me to ignore the comments of ignorant people like that trainer because they're nothing to me. She said for an adult who is supposed to be a professional, to disparage a child in front of others was absolutely disgraceful. The trainer's behavior was just a reflection of the type of person he was.

She proceeded to explain to me that I would run into people throughout my life that will tell me I can't or won't be able to do something. I had to remember that I should never let anyone put limitations on me or what I could accomplish. In the case of Jay and me, we had just scratched the surface of our potential and in time we would find out just how far we could go. She said if I really wanted to do or be something, I needed to work hard and believe in myself. If I did those things, I could achieve anything. Then she laughingly teased me by saying that included anything except singing professionally because that was definitely not a talent I was blessed with. I couldn't help but laugh and agree with her, knowing my talents were rather limited in that arena.

The following afternoon Kristine arrived to coach me. My mom filled her in on everything that happened the day before, including the comment made by the other trainer. Like my mom, Kristine was very supportive and told me to remember that although it was an "A" show, it wasn't an invitational. I had just as much right to be there as anyone else.

With both my mom and Kristine there to support me, I was finally beginning to feel more confident. That was until they moved my classes from the pony ring to the hunter ring again. As we looked at the first course, we immediately noticed that the last two jumps were an in an out with a distance of twenty-six feet between them. Kristine explained that either one of two things would happen when Jay and I got to the last jumps. In a best case scenario he would jump the first one, add a stride and do it in two instead of one. The more likely outcome would be that he'd run out before the second jump. She told me to keep my butt in the saddle and be prepared for anything going into that line. We watched as several of the other riders in my class had difficultly navigating the in and out, which set my nerves on edge. Over half added a stride or ran out, exactly the situations Kristine had warned me about.

Before I went into the ring, my mom put her hand on my leg and quickly explained that in my sport I didn't just rely on myself, I had a partner that was a living, breathing creature with a mind of its own. There would be times when I would be at the top of my game and he wouldn't; just as there would be times when he was performing at his best and I wasn't. What would make it all worth my effort would be those moments when both of us were totally in sync. It might not happen that afternoon at that show, but one day we would achieve that perfect partnership.

I entered the ring and rode the entire course up to the in and out very well with no major mistakes. All I had to do was get over the last two jumps and I was done. Jay took the first jump perfectly, took one stride and then ducked out hard to the right. Luckily I grabbed onto his braided mane as I felt him shift his weight beneath me and hung on with everything I had. In the process I lost a stirrup and my body started to tilt sideways off the saddle. All I kept thinking was, "I'm not going to fall off. I'm not going to fall off."

Off in the distance, I heard Kristine's voice calling out to me, "Don't you dare come off."

After several moments of struggling to remain seated, I was able to reposition myself in the saddle and regain my stirrup. I looked down at my hands and noticed I had ripped clumps of Jay's mane out; their remains still grasped between my fingers. At that point I was done, so I tipped my helmet to the judge and exited the ring. Not wanting to push the issue, we all decided it would be best if Jay and I scratched our other two classes. There would be plenty of shows for us to attend in the coming months and other courses to conquer.

Throughout the rest of the spring and summer we attended some schooling shows and most of the Fox Lea Farm rated shows. During that time we won several grand and reserve championships in hunters and equitation, which definitely helped boost my confidence level after the RMI disaster.

My favorite show that first summer was the Fox Lea Farm camp show at the end of July. When I had attended with Ticky a couple of years earlier I hadn't been able to participate in a lot of the fun activities they'd offered because of the situation with Marilyn. With Jay it was totally different story. Every day had a theme, like cruise day and space day, and I made sure Jay and I were appropriately decorated for each so the "color team" we were assigned to would receive points.

One afternoon they held a *Dress Your Horse As Your Favorite Disney Character* class. We had decided to dress Jay as Mr. Incredible from the recently released Disney/Pixar movie, *The Incredibles*. My mom spent several weeks before the show designing and sewing his costume, and when it was done, he really did look incredible! From his neck to his tail he was covered in a satiny "blanket" made to look like a red shirt on top with a yellow belt and black pants. Attached to his chest was a large replica of the *Incredible* logo that had been printed on poster board. On his back legs he had black "boots" and on his front, red sleeves with black "gloves." To make the costume compete, he had a black mask attached to his halter and some yellow hair coloring in his forelock.

Our barn was at the farthest end of the showgrounds, and as we made our way to the ring for the judging, people kept coming up to us wanting to see Mr. Incredible or yelling out to us how great he looked. The most popular question from our fans was what color team we were on. Of course, the other riders from the blue team that we ran into along the way were quite pleased to find out we were on the same team.

When we arrived at the arena, I was very surprised to see there were over twenty entries in the class. We all waited outside the gate so we could each enter individually. Jay and I received a resounding round of applause as we walked across to our place in line. My mom said quite a few people around the ring were commenting on Mr. Incredible; he was definitely a popular character. Once everyone was lined up, the judge walked down the line to look at each entry. Finally after much deliberation she made her decision. First place went to a little girl on a pony dressed as Little Bo Peep and one of her sheep, and second place went to a group of adults whose horses were the seven dwarves. After what seemed like an interminable amount of time, the voice over the loudspeaker announced that the third and final award went to Mr. Incredible. I was absolutely thrilled!

On our way back to the barn, people kept congratulating us and saying again how cute Jay looked. Of course the other blue team members were quite happy our team had received more points. The last time I had attended the camp show with Ticky it had been a huge disappointment for me, with Jay it was the complete opposite. I had so much fun the three days we were at the show, it more than made up for everything that had happened before!

In August my mom received an e-mail from the show management at Fox Lea asking competitors to review the circuit point totals and validate that they were correct. With a reserve championship and grand already in the Children's Hunters, Jay was in first place with 72 points, well ahead of the other horses. With two shows left in October and November, I decided my goal would be to end the circuit with Jay as the Grand Champion Children's Hunter. Knowing they also gave awards for their combined "A" and "C" circuits, my mom did some quick calculations and informed me that there was an excellent chance I could get enough points for Jay to be the year-end combined circuit Reserve Champion in the Children's Hunter 14 and Under division. That became my second goal.

This is actually a good time to explain a bit about my mom and how I'm able to share such detailed information about my show experiences. My mom works as a Telecommunications Manager for a division of a very well known Central Florida company. While much of her job is technically oriented, she is also responsible for evaluating and maintaining a lot of statistical information. Although I often tease her by saying she has obsessive compulsive disorder when it comes to stats, she will admit she truly enjoys calculating numbers and figuring things out. Her favorite math class in high school was Probability and Statistics, and to her, working with numbers is like playing a game or working on a puzzle. Amazingly, thanks to her obsession with numbers I have a detailed show record documenting all of my experiences.

It all began many years ago when I first started showing Ticky on a regular basis. Someone told my mom to keep track of his show record in case we ever decided to sell him as it would validate his asking price. From that time on, she began keeping an annual record of all my show results. She had separate sheets for rated and local show results, in addition to, sheets for circuit and association points. She had notations on everything from how many people were in the class to how high the jumps were to how much money I'd won. She'd also documented which trainer I was working with at the time of the show and special notations; like when Ticky got his leg caught in the lead rope. She also broke down my placings into percentages based on the number of classes I'd shown in. I think it's both fascinating and amusing when she starts telling me my percentages or how many points I need to secure a place in some year-end standings. She really does love that stuff!

After the Fox Lea September "A" show, she figured out how many points I would need to achieve my goals based on the point accumulations of the other horses in the divisions. At the time, I was in seventh place in the Central Florida Hunter Jumper Children's Hunter 14 and Under division and there was a good chance I could move into the top six during the last few months of the season. In addition, Jay had a commanding lead in the Performance Horse Registry's Silver Stirrups standings for the Children's Hunter division in Zone 4. It also appeared I would qualify for the Atlantic Coast League Children's Hunter Finals in North Carolina that fall. Although none of us had expected Jay and I to be in the running for any awards when we started showing that spring, I was beginning to feel extremely confident that we would finish the year in good standing.

Our plan had been to attend the CFHJA show at the end of September, the last two Fox Lea "C" shows and their November "A" show, which was also the zone finals show. At the time, Vicky, our neighbor Ernie, and my mom had all been using the same farrier for the past several years. We all really liked him a lot and he always automatically showed up every six weeks to take care of the horses. Mom would leave the gate unlocked, stick a check on the tack room door and a cooler with drinks in the wash rack before she left for work the morning he was due. When she arrived home later that day, the boys would be done. If we were having a problem with one of the horses, he'd come out when we were home and either have us move the horse around in hand or have me hop on so he could see what was going on. If one of the horses threw a shoe, he was out in no time to fix it. It was the ideal situation.

Therefore, it was quite surprising when he didn't show up in mid-September for our normal appointment. We knew he'd recently experienced a traumatic personal situation, so my mom thought maybe he'd accidentally forgotten to come out. She and Ernie both left a couple messages on his answering machine, but after a week they still hadn't heard anything from him. When my mom said something to Vicky about it, she told her he'd also been a no-show for her appointment, as well as her other friend's. She assured her she would get to the bottom of it and find out what was going on.

We were only a few days away from the CFHJA show and coming up on almost eight weeks since the last time Jay's shoes were done.

We never let him go that long between trimmings and his shoes were starting to get loose. Unless we could get them reset before the show, there was no way he would be able to jump courses. I was becoming quite concerned wondering whether we'd even be able to make it to the show.

Vicky called my mom one evening to let her in on some bad news. Our farrier had decided to quit and go back to automotive work without letting his clients know. We were all completely stunned. He'd always told my mom we were one of his best clients and she was very upset that he didn't even have the courtesy to tell us about his decision, especially when he knew I was showing on a regular basis. Of course she wouldn't have been very happy about it, but knowing the circumstances surrounding certain recent events in his life, she would have understood. We all knew the chances of getting a farrier to come out in the next day or two was going to be highly unlikely, but we had to at least try.

By the next morning, Vicky was able to provide us with a list of farriers that had been recommended by people she knew. She and my mom spent several hours calling each one to see if they could at least come out to take care of Jay. Unfortunately, they were all booked solid; we had no alternative but to scratch from the show.

Little did we know, that one incident would be the catalyst in a series of events which would define my relationship with Jay. In the coming months our trust and faith in each other would be put to the test time and again. It would also be a period in which I would repeatedly question my abilities and those of my horse.

CHAPTER 9

Jay's Unusual Behavior

Having scratched from the CFHJA show and with the October Fox Lea "C" show only a couple of weeks away, my mom wanted to make sure we had plenty of time to get Jay's feet taken care of. She made an appointment with a farrier who was recommended by the mother of one of Kristine's other students. She'd been using him for quite some time and he was a family friend. My mom would later say she should have never called him since she knew the girl's horse had been having lameness issues for months, but everyone involved said it didn't have anything to do with his hooves.

Within a couple of days the farrier came out to the house and took care of the horses without incident. He removed the steel shoes our old farrier had used on Jay's front feet and replaced them with thin aluminum ones. He told us that all of the hunter/jumpers he worked on had aluminum shoes because it made them move better. We assumed he knew what he was doing and accepted his word.

Everything seemed fine while we practiced and I eagerly looked forward to our next show. On October 14th, my mom and I headed down to Venice for the Fox Lea show. After getting everything unloaded and set up, I took Jay to the East Hunter ring where he schooled really well. I felt my goals were within my reach and I couldn't wait to compete.

The next day, after winning our first hunter over fences class, Jay started doing some weird lead change thing going into and through lines. In the past, he would sometimes incorrectly swap leads if I took a corner too sharply, pulled the reins and shifted my weight as we approached a line. That day though, you would have thought I was asking him to do one and two tempis down the lines. I was really making an extra effort to be cognizant of my position in the saddle, my hands and my track around the turns, so I was completely at a loss as to what was causing his behavior. We ended up doing okay that first day and my mom said I didn't lose much ground in the standings.

The second day was an utter disaster. Jay wouldn't listen to me and seemed overly "looky" as he went around the ring. In my first class of the day, an equitation over fences class, we placed seventh out of seven. Our next jumping class was the HBO Children's Medal. We started off surprisingly well and I was beginning to think Jay was back to normal. Then halfway through the course as we approached the first jump of a line in front of the judge, he did something to me he had never done before in the show ring, he dumped me. He gave no indication that he wasn't going to take the jump, but at the last second he ducked out to the left causing me to fall off into the flower box at the base of the jump. I remember hearing people gasp as I hit it. My mom came out immediately to make sure I was okay and some of the other trainers were nice enough to catch Jay for me. When I got back on my feet, one of them gave me a leg up so I could exit the ring on horseback.

Once outside I couldn't help myself and started crying. I was actually getting scared because I didn't know why Jay was acting that way. He hadn't done anything remotely like that in months. Panic started to overtake me as I thought about going into the ring again and I told my mom I wanted to scratch the rest of my classes. She said if that's what I really wanted to do, she was okay with it, but I had to take Jay in for one more over fence class first to show him his behavior was not acceptable. If at any point I became too scared to continue, I could stop, tip my helmet to the judge, and walk out. She said she knew it would be difficult after what had just happened, but I had to at least try. I didn't realize at the time that making me go in for my next class was as much for my benefit as it was for Jay's.

I ended up finishing my last two over fence, as well as, my two under saddle classes. I was glad though when I was done for the day. Neither my mom nor I could understand what was wrong with Jay, so we just wrote it off as what Kristine referred to as "a Jay thing" and hoped it didn't happen again.

Back at home Jay started exhibiting some equally bizarre behavior when we schooled, so my mom made the decision not to attend the Atlantic Coast League Finals even though we had qualified and had accepted. He had been so inconsistent since the October show, she didn't think putting both of us in a stressful situation in an indoor arena was the wisest course of action at that point. Kristine agreed wholeheartedly. My mom notified the League so the next person in the standings would have the chance to participate.

Since the show year was almost over, Kristine asked me what my goals were for the following year. I told her I really wanted to focus on equitation and medal classes. I would have loved to do jumpers with Jay, but I didn't think that was going to be his forte. I wanted to see how far I could go in the National Children's Medal standings and finish the year in the top ten for the HBO Children's Horse Medal. I also wanted to show in the Equitation 12-14 division to get points for CFHJA. Her response was that Jay would never be an equitation horse and we might have to look at other options if I really wanted to go in that direction. I was absolutely devastated by her comments.

Later that evening my mom told me not to be discouraged. She would find out what Jay and I needed to learn to become successful in equitation and help us practice. No one could say if he would be able to do it or not because we hadn't really tried yet. We'd held our own in the few classes we'd already participated in, so we couldn't count Jay out just yet.

My mom was on a mission. She began reading every article she could about equitation and reviewed all the tests that I could be asked to perform. She watched videos of medal finals and any other relevant shows that she thought would help. In the coming months she would watch medal classes at horse shows and try to determine the placings to see if she was consistent with the judge. It also helped her to identify things they were looking for. At the October Fox Lea show, she had been in the pavilion during one of the medal tests and had overheard the judge saying she was going to make the finalists ride with no stirrups because their legs were so weak. As soon as we got home she started making me ride without stirrups and let Kristine know we had added it to our practice routine.

Knowing she would be a nervous wreck at the November "C" circuit finals show, my mom asked Kristine to accompany us. In one of her true obsessive moments, she had a piece of paper that listed the points for each competitor and she was calculating the standings after every class. Even though Jay only placed third and fourth in each of our classes on Saturday, it was enough for us to secure the Grand Championship for the circuit. I was so excited when my name was announced over the loudspeaker the next day. I quickly made my way to the office where I was presented with my ribbon and a beautifully engraved crystal plate.

It was at that point Kristine began to strongly suggest that Jay was not the horse she'd thought he'd turn out to be. He was adding half strides in lines, jumping sideways, unexpectedly swapping his leads, and dragging his feet over jumps. My mom kept telling her that she hadn't seen him at the earlier shows when he was jumping beautifully and had been beating those same horses. Something was different; we just couldn't figure out what it could be.

The new farrier came back out to trim the boys at the end of November just before the zone finals at Fox Lea. Since my mom was working, she had my dad ask him specifically if he thought Jay needed back shoes because his hooves seemed to be breaking up pretty badly. My dad called to tell her his response had been that if it was his horse, he wouldn't put shoes on the back; so she just let it go.

Even though I was still securely holding the second place position in the combined circuit standings, my mom once again asked Kristine to join us at the show to coach me. Jay's first two classes were over fences and he was worse than he had been a couple of weeks before. Unsurprisingly, he didn't even place in either one. It wasn't until the flat class that we realized something was very wrong. As he trotted around the ring, it was obvious he was lame in front. When the class concluded and we exited the ring, Kristine checked his legs. Her best guess was that the farrier had just trimmed Jay a little too close on the front, which caused him to be ouchy. It was then she also noticed that his left hind pastern was swollen, even though he wasn't lame on that foot. She advised us we would just need to let the farrier know what was going on to ensure it didn't happen again in the future. I wish we had known it wasn't going to be that easy.

There was no alternative at that point; we had to scratch the remainder of our classes for that day and the next. We were very relieved to find out that even without being able to accumulate any additional points I had enough of a lead to hold on to the Reserve Championship for the combined circuits. For our efforts, we received a ribbon and an engraved cut crystal canister.

A few weeks later, we attended the CFHJA December awards show. Since I hadn't accumulated many points during the last few shows of the season, Jay and I didn't make the top six for the Children's Hunter division. We did finish a respectable ninth, even though we had only shown at a limited number of rated shows during the year. I was quite happy to receive the third place award for the Hunter Pleasure Horse division.

Because Jay had never been at the fairgrounds before, my mom wanted me to school him in the covered arena before the banquet Friday evening. Feeling overly confident, I told her we didn't need to. On Saturday morning she suggested I walk Jay around the grounds to acclimate him to the new surroundings. From the moment he left his stall, he acted as if he was going to explode at any minute. As he walked around the grounds, every sensor in his body seemed to be activated. I wrote it off as just being in a new environment.

At my mom's request, Kristine arrived later in the afternoon for the Children's Hunter classes. It was another complete disaster; I wasn't able to get Jay over the first jump and we were disqualified from both our over fence classes. To add insult to injury, Kristine's old boss was there coaching one of her former students in the same class. I felt as though Linda was thoroughly enjoying my misfortune. Again, we had no other choice but to scratch Jay from the rest of his classes and head for home.

By that time, Kristine was furious with Jay. She said he was never going to be the horse I needed him to be, and it would probably be best to just sell him and be done with it. My mom was so angry with him she was ready to start posting ads. The only thing that stopped her was that she kept going back to the fact that he had been doing extremely well earlier in the year.

The next weekend we were scheduled to attend the RMI show at Canterbury Showplace in Newberry. When Kristine came for my lesson during the week, she noticed that Jay's hind pastern was still swollen. The only thing we could attribute it to was the trimming. Since the RMI show always had a farrier on-site my mom decided to have him look at Jay Saturday morning; which would work out perfectly because our classes were at the end of the day. She would also ask him what he thought about putting shoes on his back feet.

As we were preparing to leave for the show on Friday, Jay decided to be goofy in the pasture and pulled one of his front shoes. We decided not to worry about it; we would have the show farrier take care of that as well. By the time we arrived at the showgrounds the sun was already beginning to set, which only gave me a little time to school. Since Jay didn't seem ouchy, I showed him the ring and worked him a little on the flat.

Early the next morning we brought Jay over to the farrier's work area. My mom introduced herself and explained what had been going on. She told him she felt Jay needed back shoes and asked for his opinion. Haws was actually shocked at what he saw when he looked at Jay's hooves. Yes, he definitely needed back shoes. In fact, all of his feet were a mess because the new farrier had literally chopped his heels down to nothing and his angles were horrible. He assured us he could fix him; wedge aluminum shoes on the front and steel on the back. It ended up taking him over two hours to get the shoes on Jay and build up his hind hooves with acrylic.

During that time, my mom and I were given an amazing education on horseshoeing. I learned about angles and what types of shoes could fix what problems. I had to admit, I'd never seen as many different types of shoes as I did in the back of the Haws' truck. By the time he was done, I truly believed him when he said he could fix any problem. I even mentioned to him that we had considered selling Jay due to recent events. He told us that it would have been a shame since "Jaybird," a nickname that would stick, was such a nice horse. After watching how painstakingly he worked and measured, there was absolutely no doubt in my mind that he really knew his stuff. Deep down, I believed that we had been sent to him for a reason.

When Haws finally finished his work, Jay's feet looked better than they had in months. It didn't take long to realize they felt better too. You could almost see the relief on his face when he started walking on his fancy new shoes. He was actually stepping out again and not taking dinky little steps. The man was truly a godsend! My mom told him as much and we both thanked him profusely for his efforts.

Several hours later as I was warming Jay up for his classes, I was amazed by the difference in his movement. Haws had asked us to let him know when we were going to warm-up so he could see how Jay was doing. Needless to say, he was very pleased with the results.

Much to everyone's chagrin, just as I was getting ready to go in for my first class, the light drizzle that had been falling all day turned into torrential rain. To make matters worse, it was only in the low 50's so the cold was absolutely bone chilling. Rather than risk injury or illness to Jay or me, we headed back to the barn. Show management waited as long as they could, but still ended up cancelling the rest of the day's classes.

The next day dawned just as dreary. My mom and I discussed the situation and decided it wasn't worth showing even if it eventually cleared up. Jay's feet were fixed and he had moved well when I warmed him up the day before. He was back to his old self; cooperative and happy. We decided to pack everything up and head home.

In a perfect world, Haws would have lived nearby and come to my house every six weeks to take care of the boys. Unfortunately, he lived over two hours and a hundred miles away. With gas prices at record levels, there was no way my parents could afford to bring Jay up to him on a regular basis. And the cost for him to drive down to us would have been several hundred dollars; something not within their budgetary constraints.

Luckily, we were able to bring Jay back up to him one more time to be re-shod at the end of January. When my mom explained her financial limitations and told him she would have to find someone closer to home, he was kind enough to provide her with all the info regarding the shoes he put on him and how they should be positioned. He also offered us his assistance if we ever needed it and said if we could set him up with a few other horse owners in the area, it would help defray the cost for him to come down to us. Sadly, we just didn't know enough people to make it worth the trip for him.

Needing to find someone closer to home, my mom decided to go with a farrier that had taken over most of Kristine students' horses rather than the new one Vicky was using. Ron had been able to fix a horse that had been lame for months and was supposed to be one of the best in Central Florida. He worked with two large well-known equestrian facilities, so my mom figured he must know what he was doing if he had been able to keep those clients for several years. Again, she would later say we should have run the other way.

CHAPTER 10

Where Has My Horse Gone?

With Jay's erratic behavior the past couple of months, my mom had suggested I modify my goals a little for the coming year. Rather than try for both Children's medals, I might want to just focus on the HBO Medal. Since those classes were offered at both the local and rated level, I could use the first few months of the year to hone Jay's and my skills at local shows while still accumulating points.

I was happy to find out that FHCA would be offering the class at their shows. They had always been some of my favorite shows to attend because the management and staff were always so friendly and supportive. We'd only attended one of their shows with Jay, nearly a year before, so I was really looking forward to seeing everyone again.

In addition to the medal, I could show in their Junior/Adult Amateur Equitation division and work toward a year-end award. Therefore, with a minor change in direction, my goals for 2006 became a top ten finish in the HBO Medal standings, the FHCA year-end Junior/Adult Amateur Grand Champion honors, and participation in the November FHCA Horseshows in the Park Medal finals.

Much to my disappointment, when I told Kristine what my new goals for the year were, she once again responded that Jay would never be an equitation horse. He just didn't have it in him. She said if I genuinely wanted to go in that direction, we should look at other options because he'd never be a serious competitor. She said he had no jumping style; he hollowed his back and inverted his neck, was inconsistent with his distances, and didn't like to snap his knees up. And that was just the beginning; she had a whole list of other issues to prove he wasn't up to the task.

I was so confused because I felt I had developed a special bond with Jay. He just hadn't been himself because of the hoof problems. I tried to ignore what she said, but I couldn't help myself and began to doubt Jay's ability. Still, I wasn't ready to give up on him.

My mom's argument was that if he was truly that bad, he wouldn't have done as well as he had the previous year in the hunters. We had to remember that most of the issues had started when we were forced to find a new farrier. She reminded me of our conversation the previous spring at our first "A" show when the trainer ridiculed Jay. She said, "Always remember; never let anyone put limitations on you, no matter who they are. You'll never really know how far you can go or what you can achieve until you try."

Jay had never even been asked to do some of the more technical maneuvers required in equitation; it would be up to us to teach him what to do. If he truly couldn't perform at the level required, we'd have to accept that, but we were both committed to doing whatever was necessary to help him succeed.

After printing out the list of tests I could be asked to perform in the medal class, my mom asked Kristine which ones she thought we needed to work on. Her response was not to worry about them; we needed to focus on other things. My mom explained to her I could be asked to do any of the listed tests in a medal class and I had to know how to perform them. She said I already knew how to do them and there were other things we needed to work on more.

My mom figured out how to help me practice most of the tests at home, but she was unsure how to train Jay to perform the turn on the haunches and turn on the forehand. When she mentioned it to Vicky, she immediately volunteered to come out one evening after work to show me what to do. After quite a few tries, and a bit of confusion on both of our parts while attempting the exercises, Jay and I finally started getting the hang of them.

One thing Vicky had noticed during our training session was that Jay could only handle so much before a switch went off in his head and he shut everything out. As my mom had become fond of saying, he would reach a point where "Jay has left the building." Vicky had worked with several other Thoroughbreds in the past and said she'd experienced that before. As such, she gave me some suggestions that would help me work more effectively when training Jay.

Most importantly, I had to avoid asking him to do the same thing over and over. Just as I would get frustrated in that type of situation, so would he. She told me to always be aware of how he's behaving when we're trying to teach him something new or practicing something specific. If I paid close attention, I'd be able to feel when he'd be getting close to his overload threshold. His muscles would become overly tense, he would be hypersensitive and start to lose focus; which in turn, would cause him to become fussy and eventually hit the breaking point. When I felt those moments coming, I should stop what I'm doing and move on to something else that he was more comfortable with for a little while to re-focus his attention. Thus, I could avoid pushing him to the point of flipping the switch and not have to deal with his out- of- body drama.

Vicky also recommended that if there was something he was having difficulty grasping, stop and let him think about it overnight. From her experience, horses sometimes needed time to get a mental grasp on what they were being asked to do. If they had a chance to think about it, they would generally come back the next day and perform whatever it was much better. She also suggested that we not try to teach him more than one new concept at a time to avoid overwhelming him.

Armed with Vicky's training advice and the knowledge of what we needed to work on, Jay and I spent hours practicing and practicing. When I felt his frustration building, we'd move on to something else and try again later. Another piece of the puzzle that was Jay had been solved. In no time, I was feeling very self-assured knowing I could complete any of the equitation tests I might be asked to perform.

Our first show of the year was a local show at Fannin Hill Farm in Brooksville on January 8th. I had to admit I was nervous about showing Jay after everything we'd gone through the past few months because I didn't know how he would behave. As a result, my body and arms were pretty stiff when I first went into the ring. After we got through our three Children's Hunter classes without incident, I finally began to relax. We ended up placing and getting good ribbons in each one.

I was feeling much more confident as I entered the ring for my Marshall and Sterling Hunter Classic. Everything was going smoothly until we got to the end of the course. On the opposite side of the arena from the in-gate was a flagpole situated between the upper and lower rings with American and Tampa Bay Bucs flags attached. The wind had gradually been picking up throughout the day, and at times, periodic strong gusts would cause the flags to flap around. Quite a few horses in both rings had spooked because of it. One young girl in the lower ring had been bucked off by her pony when they started to snap loudly in the wind as she passed by.

We were showing in the upper ring, which because of its position to the flagpole, seemed to be right on top of it. Jay and I had turned the corner by the in-gate and were making our way to the first jump of the outside line on the right in front of the judge. Jay took it perfectly and we were on our way to the second one at a nice easy pace. The flags were in front of us to the right. One stride out from the jump, a heavy wind gust picked up the flags making them wave wildly and snap loudly. Jay must have seen it the same time I caught it out of the corner of my eye. He unexpectedly slammed on the brakes and then ducked quickly to the left away from the horse eating flag monster, causing me to lose my balance and literally pop straight up out of the saddle. The funny thing was I landed standing on my feet only a few feet from the judge's stand. My mom said I looked like a gymnast who had just dismounted from the balance beam. I stood there in shock for a few seconds and when everyone around the ring realized I was okay, they all started applauding. I couldn't help myself and took a bow, which brought a round of laughter from the crowd and the judge. Jay decided to wait for me at the in-gate; so I walked over to him, hopped back on and exited the ring.

Our last class of the day was the HBO Children's Medal. It was very much like a hunter course with the exception of one rollback and a bending line. As I went over the course with my mom, I realized there was one part where I had the opportunity to impress the judge. At the end of the course you had to come off the outside line on the left at the far end of the ring, take the first jump of the inside line on the right going toward the in-gate and bend to the second jump of the other inside line. Earlier that week during my lesson, Kristine had showed me how to ride two inside jumps so you made a straight line instead of a bend. Rather than go all the way into the corner for the turn to the first jump, you turned as you were parallel to the jump and took it at an angle instead of straight on. Then you could ride directly to the second jump, taking that at an angle as well.

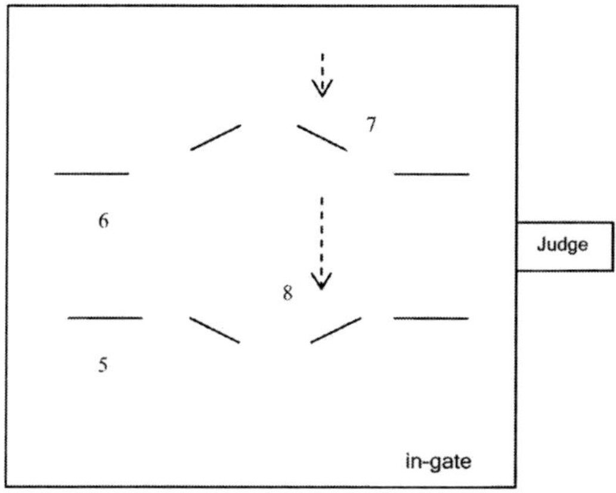

HBO Children's Horse Medal

The other riders all rode the last two jumps like a hunter course; going deep into the corner for the first one, then making a big bend to the second one. I rode it exactly as we'd practiced, going in at an angle and making a straight line from one jump to the other. It rode perfectly and we ended up winning the class!

The following weekend was the FHCA end of year show at Canterbury Showplace in Newberry. They were offering one more opportunity to qualify for all of their 2005 Hunter Invitational and Horseshows in the Park Medal finals on Friday evening, so we decided I'd enter the Children's Hunter, Regular Working Hunter and HSITP Medal qualifiers. Our only concern was that all my classes that weekend would be held in a covered arena, and the qualifiers and finals would be held at night under the lights. Although I had warmed Jay up in the covered arena at Fox Lea a couple of times, he had never shown in one before.

While Fox Lea's covered arena was basically just a roof over the ring with a judge's stand and a few bleachers outside its perimeter, Canterbury's was a more expansive facility. At the end opposite the in-gate, a glass fronted announcer's booth was centrally positioned right next to the rail. The facility's office building with several large reflective windows stood directly behind it, as well as, one of Jay's new favorite monsters to its right; a flagpole. On the left side of the ring rows of metal bleachers sat on a raised concrete foundation with stairs separating each section and a walkway that linked the in-gate side of the arena to the office area. In addition, there were several rows of seats in front of the walkway alongside the ring. Another set of bleachers stood just to the right of the in-gate.

There was no doubt in my mind that the lights were going to be huge challenge for Jay, especially since he was not at all fond of schooling in our arena at night with the lights on. He liked to worry about what might be lurking in the dark shadows of the pasture, instead of paying attention to me. The weekend would end up being another chapter of new experiences to add to the ongoing Jay saga.

We schooled in the arena on Friday afternoon and Jay immediately decided he didn't want to be anywhere in the vicinity of the announcer's booth. Nor did he like the plastic tables that were set up in the area between the rail and the metal bleachers. After numerous spooks and spectacularly huge reactions, we were finally able to school over every jump. My confidence in myself and my horse was sorely lacking as we headed back to the barn.

Our first qualifier that evening was the Children's Hunter at 2'6". Just as I had expected, Jay was not very happy about showing at night under the lights, but at least he seemed willing to cooperate. To my surprise, he was very quiet and calm during our class and we pinned second out of eleven with a score of 83. I was elated when we received our score!

Our success was not going to continue though thanks to our wonderful Florida weather. The brisk breeze that had been stirring since that morning had gradually strengthened throughout the day until it became a consistently strong wind with gusts over thirty miles per hour. Earlier in the evening tornado watches had been posted that weren't scheduled to expire until the early morning hours. To make the situation even more stressful, there were severe thunderstorms moving in and out of the area at record speeds. As a result, a thick cloud cover obliterated any light from the moon, making the area surrounding the lighted arena pitch black.

While waiting for my turn in the Regular Working Hunter qualifier at 3', a fierce thunderstorm moved in without warning. In a matter of minutes, the sky exploded with lightning and thunder, which was accompanied by howling winds and a torrential downpour. Everyone was told to dismount and get into the center of the arena for protection. The force of the wind was so strong, it was blowing rain sideways about forty feet into the arena on the side by the in-gate.

I personally hate lightning and the thought of tornadoes utterly terrifies me, so standing in an arena holding my horse with basically just a metal roof over my head while a violent storm raged on around us nearly pushed me over the edge. Much to my relief, the storm was short-lived and we were able to continue with the show.

Still anxious from the storm and the potential for more severe weather, I was unable to focus my attention on the task before me. During our Regular Working Hunter qualifier, Jay decided to go for some drama and threw in a spook as we rounded the corner by the announcer's booth. I tried to act like nothing happened, kept him moving forward and continued on my course down the outside line. Our next jump was on the inside line by the in-gate that had elaborate standards shaped like Roman columns with the words Horseshows in the Park and the FHCA logo emblazoned on them. Still a little shaken from the spook, I could feel him pull back a couple of strides before the jump. Without thinking, I looked down at the jump, which provided Jay with the perfect opportunity to duck out to the right. I quickly brought him around again and was able to get him over the second time. We only scored in the 50's and finished 4th out of five; not enough to qualify for that division.

Our last class was the HSITP Medal qualifier. After the refusal in the previous class on the HSITP jump, I wasn't committed as I approached that same jump in the medal class. I'm sure Jay sensed my insecurity, especially when I shoved him at the jump as we approached. For the second time that evening, he ducked out. When I brought him back around, I rushed him to the jump and he slammed on the brakes. After a third refusal, we were disqualified. I was so embarrassed, I just wanted to get back to the barn, put Jay up and go to bed.

The next afternoon I was scheduled to show in the Children's Hunter division. Since it was the year-end awards show, nearly every class was huge. There were nineteen riders in each of my two over fence and one under saddle classes. All I could think about was what had happened the night before. It was still extremely windy and from time to time a heavy gust would cause some of the roof panels above the arena to rattle loudly; something generally not appreciated by the horses in the ring.

Although Jay completed both of his courses with no refusals, he did hesitate at a couple of jumps and got some bad distances, so we didn't pin in either over fence class. The flat class went much better, even though we trotted right under one of the roof panels when it started banging around and Jay took a few side steps. My mom said the judge was looking right at me when it happened, but we still ended up second. While it definitely made me feel better, I was becoming very anxious about the upcoming invitational class being held that evening.

I had only qualified for the Children's Hunter Invitational which was scheduled as the first class of the night. While I should have been excited after having done so well in the qualifier class the night before, I really just wanted to get it over with. I was a bit surprised at the small turnout for the invitational classes and guessed a lot of people decided to back out because of the recent weather. Our round started off okay, but as we made our way around the course I started shoving Jay at the jumps and he refused one about halfway through. I was so stressed and frustrated with everything that had happened, I wasn't thinking and yelled out, "Get," as we approached the jump the second time. It was probably not the best decision, considering I was in a hunter class, and an invitational at that. We finished our round with no other major errors, but still placed sixth out of six. I never bothered to check to see what our score was.

The next morning we were able to get through our Regular Working Hunter division without any problems. Later, in our HBO Medal class, Jay was going around the ring nicely until we approached the second jump of the outside line going away from the gate. A gust of wind picked up the flag outside the arena right in front of us and it started flapping wildly. Jay decided to have one of his moments; spinning and blasting away to the left in an effort to distance himself from the ferocious flag monster. With eight riders in the class, we didn't even pin.

I was very disappointed with our overall performance that weekend. I wished I could trust Jay again, but it seemed like every time I did, he would have a "Jay moment" and do something unexpected. I just wanted the Jay from last summer back.

The recent flag incidents had irked my mom so much she decided her next project would be to desensitize Jay to flapping objects. She was able to find a website that had a variety of decorative flags and windsocks for sale that she felt would be perfect. She ordered an interesting combination of flags; a Mardi Gras themed one with a jester face and streaming ribbons, a winter scene with the words "Let It Snow" across the top, a Hawaiian flower theme one, and another with flowers and butterflies. She also purchased a three foot long smiling sun windsock with streamers and a giant four foot rainbow fish windsock.

Much to my dismay, my mom also purchased strings of plastic flags that she could attach to the jump poles so that they hung underneath. The first ones were triangular in shape with cute cartoon fish and underwater designs. The others were square nautical flags with various symbols on them. She was determined to make sure Jay never had an issue with a flag again. I just hoped I didn't get hurt in the process.

Once the flags and windsocks arrived, she bought wooden flagpoles that she attached about ten feet above the ground on the four light poles on either side of our arena. On the light pole at the end she attached two metal plant hangers, one for each of the windsocks. Then she taped the plastic flags to some poles and set them in the jump cups. I could only imagine what the neighbors must have thought after my mom had all her new decorations in place. Between the bright new accoutrements and our unusual jumps, I don't think any other riding arena ever looked quite as interesting.

Since we generally got a nice breeze across our pasture, it didn't take long for the new props to start snapping and blowing in the wind. None of the horses liked them at first, but after a little while they just ignored them. Jay, of course, took a bit longer to adjust than the other boys, especially when the giant fish would decide to jump out at him as we rode around the ring. He liked the moving flags under the jumps even less, but at least he was willing to jump over them. I had to give my mom credit; thanks to her idea, it didn't take long for flags to become a non-issue for Jay.

In mid-February we attended a relatively large 4-H show with Kristine and her other students. When we arrived, I was shocked to find out that the judge in my ring was my former trainer, Marilyn. I was a bit anxious about her adjudicating my classes and hoped she would be fair.

Our first class was a Hunt Seat Equitation 13 & Under on the Flat. Eighteen riders, including several of Kristine's other students, entered the ring with me. The format Marilyn used to judge the class was a bit different from any I'd experienced before. As we followed the announcer's directions to walk, trot, canter, etc, riders were eliminated individually or in small groups and asked to line up in the center of the ring. When we were down to the last few riders, we were asked to perform a couple of more tests. The remaining riders were called one a time until I was the last one, which meant I had pinned first. I was ecstatic!

I felt bad for thinking Marilyn might not treat me fairly, although she definitely made sure I worked hard for that blue ribbon. The Hunt Seat Equitation 13 & Under Over Fences class was nearly as large and we pinned fourth. Aside from one or two bad distances, Jay seemed like his old self. I ended up the reserve champion for the division and got good ribbons in my other classes.

The next weekend we showed at Barrington Hill, again with Kristine and some of her other students. I really wanted to try some jumper classes, and since there would be a significant time lapse between the jumper division and my other classes, Jay would have a bit of a break in between. We did well in the two Children/Adult Jumper classes we showed in, coming in first and second. My mom noticed that during rollbacks Jay seemed to trip all over himself, so she decided her next project would be to figure out how we could make them "prettier."

That afternoon, although we won the flat class in the Open Equitation, we pinned sixth out of six in both the Equitation Over Fences and the HBO Medal. Jay decided he didn't like a particular blue wall that had been set up in the courses and ducked out on it in both classes. His inconsistency from week to week, and even day to day, both at the shows and at home was so disheartening. And every time Jay misbehaved, Kristine had to take the opportunity to put him down. The most upsetting thing was I could tell my mom was beginning to lose confidence in him, especially after being told how inept his performance was on a regular basis. If she gave up on him, I didn't know what I would do.

CHAPTER 11

New Farrier, New Challenges

On March 3rd, Ron, the farrier recommended by Kristine and her students, came out to take care of our horses. My mom explained everything that had happened with Jay and gave him the information Haws had provided regarding the shoes. We were both taken aback when he looked at Jay's feet and started saying very detrimental things about how he was shod. My mom immediately came to Haws defense and told him what a wonderful job he had done to get him sound. Ron then proceeded to tell us that Jay's front feet were fine and he didn't need wedge shoes anymore. Since everyone had spoken so highly of him, we had to believe he knew what he was talking about.

When Kristine came out for my next lesson several days later, Jay was a flaming lunatic. The little switch in his brain went off almost immediately and he didn't seem to want to listen at all. He was charging the jumps, getting under them, chipping in or adding half strides, and then trying to run away when he landed. At one point, she told me to halt him after one of the jumps in order to try to stop him from running off. Unfortunately, when I did so he slammed on the brakes so hard, he bounced straight up in the air with all four feet off the ground; something I was completely unprepared for. As a result, I lost my balance, went flying through the air, and hit the ground so hard on my lower back that the wind was knocked out of me.

I refused to admit it to my mom or Kristine, but that was the first time I was ever really afraid of Jay. He couldn't seem to focus on anything. It was as if he was a giant bundle of nerves waiting to implode and there was nothing I could do to stop it. I really had no desire to get back on him, but knew I had to. My mom brought Jay back to me and gave me a leg up. I could feel her hands shaking as she did so, but aside from asking me if I was okay, she didn't say anything.

As Jay and I started to walk around the arena, Kristine realized how scared I was and called me over to offer some consolation. I was still shaking and my eyes were burning as I sat on Jay looking down at her.

She looked up at me and said, "Let me put this into perspective for you. Does it take courage to throw a football?"

I quietly replied, "No."

"Does it take courage to shoot a basketball?"

"No."

"Does it take courage to hit a baseball?"

"No."

"Does it take courage for someone to get on a 1200 lb. horse that they've just fallen off of; a horse that's over ten times bigger than they are, has a mind of its own, and has the potential to seriously hurt them?"

I just shrugged and looked away.

She put her hand on my boot, told me to look her in the eyes, and said, "Alyx you are one of the bravest, most dedicated students I've ever had. I know what a scary feeling it is to get back on a horse that's acting like Jay is tonight, but let me tell you, that's courage. Don't you ever forget that or let anyone tell you otherwise."

Kristine's words helped relax me enough to do a little more work with Jay before my lesson was over and we were able to finish on a good note. There was definitely a lot of tension in the air as we made our way back to the barn. My mom didn't acknowledge what had happened or say anything about it; knowing my mom, that was a bad sign. I was afraid the night's episode might just prove to be Jay's ticket to a new owner.

Later that evening we sat down to discuss what had happened. She told me that since Jay was my horse and I had to ride him, it was my decision whether to keep him or not. If at any time though, she heard me say the words "I'm afraid of Jay," he would be sold. In the coming months there would be quite a few incidents that would cause her to ask me if I was afraid of him, and my response would always be "no." He might scare me with some of his antics, but aside from that one episode, I was never afraid of him.

That feeling was put to the test a couple of nights later as I prepared Jay for a horse show. It was a Friday night and we were planning to go to a show the next morning. I was in the wash rack clipping Jay's face while my mom cleaned stalls for me. I had finished his whiskers and was ready to move on to his ears. He always hated getting his ears done, so normally my mom would twitch him for me. That time I decided I wanted to try to clip his ears without the twitch and make the process less stressful for him.

I took my time with his right ear and was able to get most of it done. He wasn't happy about it, but was willing to tolerate it. We got to a point though when he decided he'd had enough, so I asked my mom to twitch him for me. She did as I asked, and while I held the twitch, she quickly finished his ear.

When she was done, she moved the mounting block over to his left side to start the other ear. While she clipped, I stood next to her on the ground still holding the twitch. For whatever reason, he was always much more sensitive about his left ear and even with the twitch he was a bit fussy. Halfway through the clipping, his switch must have engaged. Suddenly, without warning, Jay threw himself backward in the crossties, nearly sitting down. As he went back, he ripped the twitch out of my hands, whacked the clippers out of my mom's hand and nearly knocked her off the mounting block. The next thing I knew, he was leaping forward and to the left; straight at me. I jumped back as quickly as I could, but the end of my left foot didn't make it off the concrete and Jay's hoof came down on my toes. The pain was excruciating and I fell backward, unable to put any weight on my foot.

Thankfully we tie the nylon straps in the wash rack to the metal rings in the concrete with bailing twine. As he leaped forward, one side broke, allowing Jay relief from the pressure on his halter. He stood in the wash rack quivering, while I cried in agony.

My mom helped me to the house where she gingerly removed my boot to reveal hideously swollen toes that were already turning lovely shades of blue, purple and black. She tried to get me to put ice on them, but even that was too painful. She quickly ran back outside to let Jay out into the pasture, before loading me into car for a trip to the emergency room.

After waiting for a seemingly interminable amount of time, we were ushered into an examination room, and shortly thereafter, the x-ray room. Upon our return to the exam room, the doctor showed us the film explaining that the bone at the end of my big toe had literally snapped in half when Jay landed on it. The good thing was it was a very clean break and the bone would heal itself; I would just have to wear an open "bootie" for about a month. Not a trendy fashion statement, but it would do the job. Riding, of course, was out of the question until I could get back into regular shoes.

To say my mom was upset with Jay for the toe incident would have been an understatement. She must have asked me if I was afraid of him at least a dozen times within the first twenty-four hours. I knew she had almost reached a point where she'd tell me to pack his horsey bags and send him on his way, but I was determined not to let that happen.

I was so relieved when she came in from the barn one evening a couple of days after the accident stating that she knew why Jay had been behaving the way he had. When she'd pulled him up to the wash rack to groom him, the minute his front feet hit the concrete he was very tentative and seemed ouchy. She was absolutely livid when she picked up his feet to look at his hooves. Apparently, Ron had decided to replace Jay's thick wedge shoes with extremely thin, flat ones. In a matter of minutes, she was on the phone making arrangements to bring Jay back up to Haws.

The next time Ron came out, my mom firmly told him what type of shoes she wanted on Jay. She explained what had happened with regard to my accident and said he was not to take the wedges off him unless she said to. Supposedly, he couldn't find the same brand that Haws used, but eventually did find something similar that was acceptable.

The first show I was finally able to attend after the accident was at Fannin Hill Farm on April 8th. At that point, I only had a meager 11.5 points and the chances of attaining my goal of being a top ten rider in the HBO Medal standings seemed impossible. I wasn't about to give up though and said I would do whatever I had to in order to get there. Knowing how determined I was, my mom promised to spend the rest of the spring and summer months bringing me to as many shows as feasibly possible in an attempt to catch up to the top riders. We ended up attending all of the shows in the Barrington Hill and FHCA circuits, in addition to most of the Fox Lea Farm shows. It didn't take long for the show management at these events to find out what I was striving toward, and they were all very supportive.

One thing that had always been a top priority for my mom when we attended horse shows was ensuring we were friendly in our dealings with show management and staff. She loved to observe people when we went places, and over the years we'd seen some very rude and ugly behavior by trainers, riders and parents at shows. As such, from the very beginning she'd tried to foster positive relationships with the various show staffs; we were always polite to everyone, we made sure I was at the ring when I was supposed to be, and we were flexible and understanding when things didn't go as planned. She always said she never wanted anyone to see us at a show and say, "Oh no, here come those Swanhalls."

We averaged about two shows a month from April through August and I usually pinned in the top three, even in some pretty big classes. Each Friday when the Marshall and Sterling office posted the results, my mom would check to see where I was in the standings. Every week at my lesson she'd tell Kristine what position I'd moved up to. I knew Kristine always wanted me to do well, but there were times that summer I felt she didn't think I'd make it to the top ten. We all realized it wouldn't be easy since the kids up North had tons of shows they could attend in July and August, while my options in Florida were extremely limited. Yet I couldn't worry about whether anyone thought I could do it or not; I had to stay focused on my goal. As my mom said, "Keep your eye on the prize." And that's what I did.

Two times that summer Jay lost a shoe the day we were headed to a show. Both times we had to have the farrier at the showgrounds put it back on. We were a little shocked when we were told not once, but twice that our farrier wasn't doing a good job and didn't' know how to put wedge shoes on. When one offered to come do our horses for us, we just assumed he was looking for more business and pretty much blew him off. Little did we realize, he was actually trying to help us.

Unfortunately, everything seemed to fall apart just as I was closing in on my goal. On August 3rd my dad arrived home from work unexpectedly before noon. At first I thought he might be sick, but then he told me his company had let him go. He called my mom and told her the bad news. He had been working the last four years as the General Manager of a retail appliance store, and between the slowdown in the economy and his company's decision to build another location a short distance from his store, sales during the last six months had been way down. It had gotten so bad there had been days when he could count on one hand the number of people who walked in the door. We were all devastated.

When the standings were updated the very next day, I had moved up to twelfth place and still had quite a few points that hadn't been added yet. I was sure I was going to make it into the top ten; it as a bittersweet triumph.

My mom, of course, took charge of the unfortunate situation we found ourselves in and figured out ways we could cut costs. She said we'd be okay for a while and there was no need to panic. When Kristine found out, she immediately said she wouldn't charge us for lessons; she could wait until my dad got a new job and everything stabilized. I can't imagine there are many trainers out there that would do something like that, and we were all very appreciative.

One subject that came up was the number of horses we had. Back in April we had sold Ticky to a wonderful family in Palm Beach Gardens who absolutely adored him. That left us with Bo, Cheyenne, Riley, and Jay. Did we really need four horses? I sat down with my mom and dad one evening to talk about what to do.

There was no chance that Bo or Cheyenne would ever be sold; at their ages, there was no guarantee they wouldn't end up in a bad place. That left Riley and Jay. Riley still needed some fine tuning on his training, but he had a ton of potential. Although I had been doing well with Jay the past few months, he remained inconsistent a lot of the time. What's more, Kristine continued to voice her concerns regarding Jay's ability to excel as an equitation horse. Based on all that, we made the difficult decision to put him up for sale in mid-August. Our only stipulation was that Jay couldn't leave our farm until the end of the Marshall and Sterling season in early September.

While the thought of selling Jay broke my heart, I realized I couldn't be selfish and had to let him go. My parents had sacrificed so much for me over the years without complaint, selling him was a way for me to give back to them and help our family during that difficult time. Jay was the most valuable and marketable horse we owned; therefore, I knew he was the logical choice to sell. That knowledge didn't make it any easier for me.

Within two weeks a girl about my age had come out to the house with her mother and trainer to try him out. They were very interested in purchasing him and wanted to set up a vet check as soon as possible. In the interim, my mom had also been contacted by a woman who would be attending the upcoming Barrington Hill show and wanted to watch me ride Jay in my classes. A friend of hers was quite familiar with him since she'd seen him at numerous shows, and when she'd heard he was for sale, suggested the woman contact us because she thought he would be a perfect fit for her daughter. In addition, Kristine was receiving e-mails almost daily requesting more information on Jay. It was very disconcerting for me to hear about all the people who were interested in buying my horse. I was absolutely miserable knowing our partnership would probably be coming to an end very soon.

No matter how I finished in the standings, we'd already decided back in July that I wouldn't take Jay up to the Marshall and Sterling Finals. It wasn't worth spending all that money to drive him over a thousand miles to an unfamiliar venue, when he continued to behave inconsistently and erratically at showgrounds he'd been to a dozen times. Even so, my mom had said she would bring me up to the awards ceremony if I made the top ten, but that didn't seem very likely anymore.

While my dad searched for a new job, I attended the last couple of shows with medal classes. As of the August 25th update I had moved into ninth place. We still had one show left to go, and I sincerely hoped I could hang on to my position in the standings.

We ended up placing third in our last class of the year on September 2nd at a local farm show. I had accumulated a total of 94 points and hoped it would be enough to keep me in the top ten. Although one rider got within one point, I held my position and finished the year in 9th place out of nearly 400 young riders across the nation. I was also the top ranked rider from Florida.

My mom felt it was very important that I be able to attend the awards ceremony, even with everything that had happened at home. She invited Kristine to join us on the trip to New York during the finals weekend and made plans for us to do some sightseeing in the area while we were up there.

Sitting in the saddle, determined to remember everything my trainer taught me as I wait to enter the ring for my first leadline class in October 1995.

Showing in Short Stirrups with Tic Toc in 2001.

This was the first time Riley let me get close enough to pet him; I couldn't resist and had to give him a kiss.

Giving Bo a huge hug while he and Cheyenne are in the backyard eating grass.

Visiting with Margie Engle after the 2002 Budweiser American Invitational.

Showing in a hunter class with Chance at Fannin Hill Farm.

The expression of sheer joy after winning a jumper class with Tic Toc!

Receiving the best present ever on Christmas Eve 2003!

Receiving the 2004 Florida Hunter Classic Association Winter Series High Point Child Rider Award.

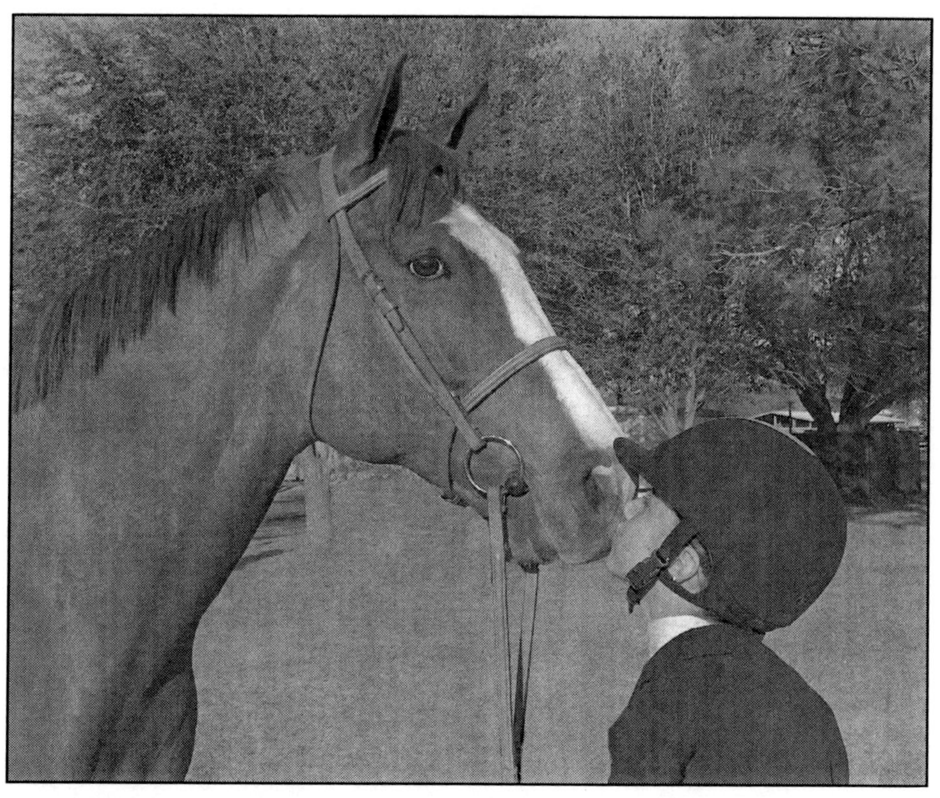

A big kiss for Jay after competing in his very first horse show in January 2005.

Jay as Mr. Incredible!

Doing some flatwork with a five year old Riley; it's hard to believe this was once the fuzzy, skinny little foal from Canada with the bad cold!

Schooling in the Grand Prix ring (center) at HITS on the Hudson during the 2007 Marshall and Sterling Finals.

Posing with Corey (center) and another rider (right) after receiving the 2007 Marshall and Sterling Children's Horse Medal Year-End Grand Champion Award.

Standing at the in-gate anxiously awaiting our turn to enter the ring for our Medal Final. (Roger Ratzenberger Photography)

Jay and I leaving the Grand Prix ring after completing our round. (Roger Ratzenberger Photography)

Hanging out and having fun with my mom after the show. (Roger Ratzenberger Photography)

CHAPTER 12

A Turning Point

We knew it would take at least six months to get Riley up to 3', so I wanted to accumulate as many Marshall and Sterling points as possible early in the season in case we sold Jay. As it turned out, the first show of the new Marshall and Sterling season at Barrington Hill on September 9th proved quite interesting, and everyone's emotions were running high. In addition to bringing Jay for the Open Equitation and Medal, Riley and I were entered in our first classes together in the Pre-Greens. Kristine and some of her other students also planned on attending the show, which made my mom more comfortable; especially since she knew it would be an anxious day for me.

My stress level quickly elevated as soon as we arrived because Riley was a very happy boy when he got off the trailer. His Warmblood brain kicked in after about five minutes though and he was back to his "whatever" mode. I wished I could have said the same for me. For some reason I always expected him to have "Jay moments," even though Riley had never done anything even remotely close to what he had. To top it off, we were running late and my mom didn't have enough time to lunge Riley as she had planned. As we tacked him up, I kept asking her if he would be okay. She assured me he would be fine and told me to just take him in the ring.

Of course, the minute we started walking away, Jay had to start calling for his best friend. My mom asked my dad walk him under the trees and let him eat grass in an attempt to distract him while I schooled Riley. She knew that Jay's whinnying would bother me more than it did him.

Kristine was already down by the lower ring schooling some of her younger students, so I headed to the upper ring with Riley while my mom set off to let her know we'd arrived. She mentioned to her that I was a very stressed out and then let her take over. Riley handled schooling like an old pro and could have cared less that Jay was calling to him every few minutes. Since time was running out before the start of the show, I had to quickly get out of the ring and switch horses. While my parents got Riley set up in his stall, I schooled Jay. Once I finished with him, the waiting game began.

I really enjoyed going to shows at Barrington Hill. The grounds were very nice and we usually parked the trailer close to the ring so we could hang out and watch the show. It was the ideal set up; all we had to do was provide Jay with hay and water at the trailer, open the awning, put out some chairs, sit back and relax. With Riley safely ensconced in his stall up at the barn, we were all set.

Riley's classes would be up first; two over fences at 2'3" and a flat. Knowing I was a bit concerned that I'd have to show him over fences first, my mom suggested we enter him in the Hunter Pleasure Horse class because it would run earlier. I was definitely up for that, and as we reviewed the prizelist further, we noticed they'd added a bareback "sit a buck" class. That sounded like fun, so I eagerly told my mom I'd like to do the class with Jay. Teasingly she said I'd probably be the only one it, but if nothing else, it would allow the judge to see how I rode.

As we prepared Riley for his classes, she reminded me that we weren't there to win ribbons with him. It was our first show together, and she just wanted me to feel comfortable and make it a good experience for both of us. We all agreed Riley was not necessarily built to be a hunter, but there were no lower level equitation classes that she could put us in; therefore, Pre-Greens was our only option. She told me to just ride them like equitation classes.

There ended up being only one other rider in the Hunter Pleasure class. I knew my position was stiff and inflexible, as if I was waiting for Riley to do something, but I couldn't help myself. I thought I was keeping him collected, but I was actually hanging on with everything I had. To Riley's credit, he just went around doing whatever I asked. Once it was over and I realized he wasn't going to be "bad," I began to look forward to our other classes.

My next class was the bareback class, and as predicted, I was the only one in it. Kristine had gone to the warm-up area to work with one of her other students, so it was the Alyx and Mom team. My mom told the gate person that I was okay doing the class by myself if the judge didn't mind. The judge agreed, so Jay and I entered the ring with a dollar nestled securely under my leg. She really put us through our paces; walk, posting trot, sitting trot, canter, hand gallop, and halt. Yet after all the flatwork, the dollar was still positioned snugly where it started.

The really cool thing was that as the class progressed, more and more people moved up to the ring to watch. Finally, after having no other options left, the announcer's voice came over the loudspeaker stating that if I felt comfortable, I could jump the first obstacle of the line in front of the judge. I had hoped they would ask me to jump, so I eagerly headed straight for the first jump. The audience grew silent as I approached, cleared it without issue, and then proceeded to the second jump in the line. For whatever reason, I thought she said to jump the entire line, not just the first jump. Again, we jumped it easily, but after Jay landed and swapped his lead, the dollar slipped out from under my leg. As I rounded the corner I realized it was gone, signaling the end of the class. When I turned back to find the missing bill, everyone was cheering for me! The announcer congratulated me on the judge's behalf for a great job. The experience was a huge confidence builder!

The Pre-Green division with Riley was next, so my mom had him tacked up and ready for me. I was extremely thankful that he just went around the ring as if he'd been doing shows for years, although I was admittedly still a little anxious. Even though he was a bit sticky and we had to do a couple of simple lead changes, we ended up with a fourth and fifth in the over fences classes out of eight. In the under saddle class I confused him with my cue and he accidentally picked up the wrong lead in one direction, but we still got a fifth in that class as well. I was quite pleased with the results and felt the judge had been very fair considering some of the mistakes we'd made.

Shortly thereafter, it was time for Jay and me to prepare for our classes. Kristine was assisting her other students, so my mom decided to school me over a few jumps herself. He was still being very cooperative and willing, so we headed up to the ring to wait. Kristine joined us, and as we stood watching the hunter rounds a woman approached us. She introduced herself as the one who had contacted my mom because she was interested in Jay for her daughter. She proceeded to explain to us that she had been looking for us all day, but hadn't been able to track us down. Evidently she didn't realize that I had ridden Jay in the bareback class and had missed watching him go.

Kristine gave her a quick overview of Jay's background. When she finished, the woman motioned down to the other ring where her daughter was "testing" another horse in a Beginner Hunter class and said that she thought that horse would be more suitable. We assured her it was not a problem and told her we hoped it worked out for her. As the woman walked away, I thought my mom caught a glimpse of the panicked look I had on my face before I could hide it. I knew it would be a deciding day for me, one way or the other.

By the time Jay's classes started, my legs were literally shaking in the stirrups. I had definitely overdone it earlier and was really starting to feel it in my muscles. We placed third in both the Open Equitation Over Fences and on the Flat. Even though my mom felt bad about asking me to do it, she had me take Jay over a couple of 3'6" jumps in the schooling area to remind him to pick up his feet for the medal class.

My mom seemed to know that with everything that had been going on the past few weeks and the pressure of having Kristine at the show, I was a bit more nervous than usual, wanting to make sure I didn't make any mistakes. In an effort to alleviate some of my tension, she reminded me that I had finished the year as the top ranked Florida rider for the HBO Medal and had already proven what I could do. She said I didn't have to catch anybody; they had to try to catch me. It definitely made me feel better.

I didn't know why, but I always felt more stressed out when Kristine was at a show with me. I couldn't stop myself from getting worked up because I felt I had to do everything perfectly when she was there. It was something that seemed to intensify after our disastrous performance in front of her former boss the previous December. That being said, I was much more relaxed when it was just my mom and me. Even though she acted as my trainer at shows, she always told me the two most important things were too have fun and be safe. Of course, my mom wanted me to do well, but it was never about the ribbons. She often told me, "As long as you do your best, that's all anyone can ask of you."

Whenever something didn't go as planned in a class, she'd remind me that every time I went into the ring it was a learning experience. During a medal class at a Fox Lea show the previous summer, I had been confused by the judge's instructions for a test and was repeatedly unable to pick up a counter canter as directed. She'd immediately sensed my frustration and embarrassment as I exited the ring, so she suggested that I watch the other three riders who were testing go to see how they handled the situation. As we observed the other competitors, she explained that riders at every level make mistakes, but the ones who were consistently successful over time were the ones who learned from their errors. When the other riders finished their rounds she asked me what I'd learned from their rides and what I would do differently if I had to ride the same test again. As always, she found a way to put a positive spin on the situation, which inevitably made me feel better about it.

Kristine was coaching another student and wasn't at my ring when Jay and I went in for our medal class. Although our round was pretty good, Jay chipped into the first jump of an inside line and we got a bad distance into the second one which placed us second going into the test. The judge called the top riders back into the ring and asked us to face her. She proceeded to explain the test and asked if we had any questions. One of her directions was to remain facing her so we wouldn't be able to see what the other competitors were doing.

When my turn came, I followed her instructions exactly; I trotted the first jump, hand galloped to the second, made a bending line to the third, halted on the far side of the ring, backed three steps, and walked back to the line with a loose rein. Jay seemed to know exactly what I wanted him to do before I even asked. I hoped it looked as effortless as it felt. The rider that was in first place tested next. She started off well, but my mom said later she didn't change her position or open her horse's stride for the hand gallop, rubbed a rail and had a bit of a rough halt; all of which bumped her down in the placings and me up to first. I was so happy I couldn't contain the enormous grin on my face when I left the ring.

Back at the trailer, my mom said we needed to talk about the Jay situation. While I was untacking him, she told me how pleased she was with him and what a wonderful job he'd done for me. I felt tears well up in my eyes as I came to the realization that Jay and I may have just competed in our last show together. I tried to hide my face so my mom wouldn't see me cry. Then unexpectedly, she quietly asked me if I wanted to keep him. My reply was a very loud and emphatic, "Yes!" Smiling at my exuberant response, she assured me that if it was what I really wanted, she would find a way to make it work. She appreciated the fact that I had been willing to give up my beloved horse to help our family, but knowing how much I cared about him and what we'd been through together, she felt it was more important to do everything possible to keep us together.

As we had discussed numerous times in the past, her main concern was whether or not I was afraid of Jay. There had been quite a few times when he had done things that had literally terrified her; both when I was riding him and on the ground. I assured her that I was not afraid of him, but admitted that sometimes she and Kristine made me think badly of him because of the things they said. We discussed the comments that had been made about Jay during the past months and agreed that they would have to stop immediately. She said she would let Kristine know what I had decided later and remove his listings from the Internet.

While we were talking, a rumbling had begun in the distance and we could see a nasty thunderstorm was rolling in from the west. We quickly hosed Jay off and ran to pack everything in the trailer. Once Jay and Riley were loaded, my mom and I headed to the barn for a quick bathroom run before we left. While waiting for my mom, I started talking to a lady in front of the barn, not realizing at first that it was the judge. My mom walked over to us as the judge mentioned she thought she recognized me from the Pre-Green Hunter classes as the rider whose trainer questioned my placings. I quickly let her know that was not me; the rider she was referring to one of Kristine's other students. I reminded her that I was the rider on the big black horse in the Pre-Greens and the lone rider in the bareback class. The judge immediately remembered me, and to my utter delight, complimented me on my riding. When she found out it was my first show with Riley, she told me that I'd handled him very well and encouraged me to keep working on his canter departures and lead changes.

The judge proceeded to tell me she had been very impressed with my performance in the bareback class. She said that after I had done all the flat work, she'd asked the announcer on the radio if she thought I would be comfortable taking a jump. The announcer had replied she didn't see why not since my legs looked so strong. I explained to her it was because my mom made me practice without stirrups on a regular basis. The judge seemed to really appreciate that and said we should have seen the other riders' faces during the Equitation on the Flat class when she'd asked them drop their irons. We all laughed when I said I actually preferred riding without stirrups. Once again, she complimented me on my performance.

By the time we left, I was beside myself with happiness. In the span of just hours, my self-confidence level had risen to incredible heights and there was no doubt in my mind I could accomplish any goal I set for myself. We were certainly off to a promising start for the 2007 season and I was hopeful it was a sign of things to come.

On the way home, my mom called Kristine and left her a message to let her know I had decided to keep Jay. When she returned her call, my mom discussed the disparaging comments that had been made about him. They agreed that the "slamming" of Jay would have to stop as it directly affected my confidence in both my horse and myself. We still had some work ahead of us to make him a consistent equitation horse, but we all agreed we were willing to put in the effort.

Interestingly, the woman that had pretty much written Jay off as an option for her daughter called Kristine right after the show to ask if she could come out to see him with her daughter and trainer. Since Kristine had already gotten our message she told her I had decided to keep him. Apparently she was rather disappointed to hear he was no longer for sale.

After unloading Jay at home and putting him in his stall so he could eat his dinner, I gave him a huge hug and told him we weren't going to sell him. As long as he did his job and took care of me, everyone would be happy. I could almost see a sense of relief wash over his face and his whole body seemed to relax. Remarkably we would soon discover something very special had happened that day, and although no one could put their finger on it, my relationship with Jay reached a whole new level.

The following morning my mom, dad and I packed Jay up for the FHCA show at Canterbury. Normally we would leave at the crack of dawn to get to the showgrounds before the classes started so I could school him over the jumps in the ring we'd be showing in, but I had decided Jay had to learn to go into any ring and do his job without seeing the jumps ahead of time. It would be interesting to see how he would react without being schooled in the covered arena before our classes.

Since we had only been able to hose Jay off the previous day due to the incoming thunderstorms, my mom and I wanted to give him a quick bath when we arrived at the showgrounds. On the way over to the wash racks we ran into one of Kristine's former students who was attending the show with her new trainer. We chatted for a few minutes and she told us she was a bit anxious because it was her first time showing in the 2'9" division. I told her not to worry, she'd do great.

As Jay and I warmed up for our classes, the girl and her trainer joined us in the schooling ring. When the girl did not perform something she wanted, the trainer immediately began yelling at her. I could see her shutting down each time a tirade began. It reminded me of my experiences with Marilyn; I knew exactly what she was going through and truly felt sorry for her. I couldn't help but comment about it to my mom as we left the ring.

Our first round was a Schooling Hunter class and our only purpose in entering it was to allow us to see how Jay would behave going into the ring cold. He surprised us all when he went over everything without any concern, although a couple of his jumps were a bit off balance. What a shock when he pinned second out of six! Our next class was the Junior/Adult Amateur Equitation Over Fences. Going into the show I was leading the division standings for the year-end award, so I really wanted to do well. I felt we rode the course nicely, especially when we did an amazingly tight rollback that no one else even attempted. The judge rewarded our effort with a first place ribbon.

Next we entered the ring for our Equitation on the Flat class. Just as we were asked to execute the posting trot, the sky exploded with what seemed like a monsoon! The noise from the rain pounding on the arena's metal roof was so loud no one could hear the announcer over the loudspeakers. The other riders and I just kept trotting and trotting and trotting. My legs were already sore from the bareback class the day before and I was struggling to keep them in the proper position. Eventually one of the show staff was able to convey to us that the judge wanted us to walk, which we continued to do until the storm eased up. It was definitely a relief when the class was over and I was glad to have at least placed third out of six.Thankfully I was able to get a little break before my medal round.

For the medal class, the final instruction noted on the posted course stated we had to canter the last jump and exit the ring at a sitting trot. When one of the riders finished the course and added a courtesy circle at the end, my mom made a point to tell me not to do the same thing; just jump the last obstacle, bring Jay back and sit trot to the gate. I assured her I wouldn't make the same mistake.

I ended up being the last rider to go and we rode the course beautifully. As my mom told me later, she knew I had won the class after we took the last jump. That was until; I cantered past her and completed a courtesy circle at the sitting trot before exiting the gate. When she asked why I had done the courtesy circle after we had discussed the other rider's mistake, I told her I didn't remember her saying not to do one. I was dead serious. She just laughed and told me it must have been the sun and heat from the day before that fried my brain a bit. Even with the faux pas at the end, the judge appreciated the rest of my ride and placed me second. My mom decided that in the future, unless absolutely necessary, she would avoid scheduling two different shows on back to back days; famous last words.

CHAPTER 13

Goals for the New Year

Our trip up to New York for the Marshall & Sterling awards party started off on a great note when, just a few days before we left, my dad got a new job as the manager of a retail chain store near our house. It wasn't what we had hoped for, but it was certainly better than nothing.

On Friday morning, September 15th my mom, Kristine and I boarded a plane bound for Albany, New York. At the last minute my mom had been able to get a reservation at the Fairlawn Inn in nearby Hunter, a beautifully restored Victorian bed and breakfast. It was about an hour away from the showgrounds, but we were thankful to have found it on such short notice.

We decided to stop at the showgrounds on our way to the inn to pick up our tickets for the Year-End Awards Party that evening. When we arrived we found out it had been raining for the past several days, so the grounds were a soupy, muddy mess. In the show office we met Patti, who gave us our party tickets and verified that I had held onto my position in the standings. I was so relieved. She was actually working on the putting the award certificates that would be presented to the top riders in their silver frames when we arrived and just happened to have mine in front of her. I was so excited I wanted to jump up and down in sheer happiness!

Patti then advised us that due to the wet conditions at the showgrounds, the evening's festivities were being relocated to Tom Struzzieri's home a short distance away. All we had to do was come back to the showgrounds that evening and buses would be provided to transport us to the party.

Since my mom and I had never been to the HITS Saugerties facility before, we decided to walk around and check everything out. I was curious to see the Grand Prix ring I'd heard so much about. As we walked up the grassy slope between the schooling rings, the massive arena unfolded before me. I'd never seen anything like it before! Surrounded by a stone wall and grassy berm on all four sides, the behemoth referred to as Grand Prix ring was larger than any I had seen before. It was absolutely awesome! I laughingly told my mom and Kristine that Jay would probably collapse from exhaustion if he had to navigate a course in there! As we watched a few rounds, I began to think to myself that Jay and I could do that. The more we watched, the more resolute I became; I was going to compete in that ring with Jay next year.

After checking out some of the stores, we stopped at a local diner for lunch and then headed to the inn so we could rest for a little while and change before the festivities that night. When we arrived back at the showgrounds, we were able to get on one of the first buses leaving for the party. There was an air of excitement among the passengers as we approached our destination on a long, winding driveway. As we exited the bus, we took a moment to observe the beautiful surroundings. Tom's house was situated on a hillside overlooking the Hudson River; the view was absolutely spectacular and the grounds were impeccably maintained. Across from the house, tents and tables had been set up for Tavern on the Green to serve their delectable culinary delights. Everything around me exceeded any expectation I'd had, and I knew it was going to be a very special evening.

With filled dinner plates and cups in hand, my mom, Kristine and I walked down the stairs built into the hillside to the pool area overlooking the river. We found an empty table and chairs on the patio where we sat down to eat our dinner. A tent with rows of folding chairs in front of it had been set up on the opposite side of the pool. We soon found out it was where they would be presenting the year-end awards and where the evening's entertainment would perform.

As the night wore on, people began making their way down to the pool area for the awards ceremony, so we secured three chairs in the front row. Finally, the moment I had been waiting for arrived and the presentations began. As each division was announced, the individual winners were called up to receive their prizes. In the medal divisions, each rider was awarded a large gold fringed ribbon and a framed certificate like the ones we had seen in the office earlier. In addition, the Grand Champion for the year also received an embroidered jacket and a gift certificate.

I could barely sit still by the time they started announcing the awards for the HBO Children's Horse Medal. When I was called up to receive my award, I was shaking with excitement. I had really done it! Even with all the setbacks I'd faced during the past year I'd achieved my goal of finishing in the top ten! When I returned to my seat, my mom gave me a big hug and told me how proud she was of me.

We decided to leave shortly after the awards presentation concluded because the inn was so far away. On our bus ride back to the showgrounds, my mom asked me what my goals would be for 2007. I responded without hesitation that I wanted to be the Marshall and Sterling Children's Medal Year-End National Grand Champion and compete in next year's finals. When she asked why, I said I really wanted the jacket! She couldn't help but smile as she told me it would be cheaper just to buy one. All kidding aside, she assured me she would do everything within her power to get me to as many shows as feasibly possible so I could accrue points.

Since my dad's new job only paid him a little more than half of what he made before, she said we'd have to play it smart when planning what shows to attend so we could stay within our now extremely limited budget. I'd finish up the equitation division for the 2006 FHCA circuit, but after that I'd show exclusively in the Marshall and Sterling Medal classes and a warm-up class or two. Our plan to limit the number of classes I showed in would also ensure that we didn't overwork Jay. His welfare and health were our top priorities and we didn't want to push him too hard just to get points.

We could also save money by only getting a stall for Jay when absolutely necessary; which wouldn't be a problem because he actually seemed to prefer hanging out next to the trailer with us. If anyone could find ways to cost effectively allow me to achieve my new goals, it was my mom. I had complete faith in her. I knew we'd all have to give up things throughout the year to make it happen, but that didn't matter; I was willing to do whatever I had to and I appreciated the fact that my parents were willing to do so as well.

My mom suggested I set a goal to accrue 200 points for the year. She believed it was something I could definitely achieve since I had been able to accumulate over 80 points in only five months. The girl who had just won the Grand Championship in the Children's Horse Medal division had done so with 149. The adult medal rider had the highest number of points totaling 178. She didn't think anyone had ever broken the 200 mark for the medals, so I would be the first.

Together we decided I would actually have two point goals for the year. The first goal would be to strive for at least 100 points from the beginning of September through the first weekend in March. That time frame would put us at the halfway mark for the show year. The next step would be to focus on accumulating another 100 points from the second weekend in March through the beginning of September. By setting my goals in six month increments the prospect of accruing 200 points didn't seem quite as overwhelming.

Then my mom gave me some very good advice that would become one of the crucial factors in helping me succeed. She explained that while Jay might not be the most expensive, or what some would consider, the fanciest horse; nor was he the type of horse that would just pack me around, he was willing to work with me and really tried to do his best for me. The last shows we'd attended were a true testament to that statement. She reminded me that I knew my horse better than anyone, so I knew what he was capable of. With that in mind, I could gain an advantage by being bold and "wowing" the judges with my riding skills rather than posing my way around the ring like some equitation riders. She said there were definite advantages to having to make tight turns and take jumps at sharp angles in our arena at home. But most importantly, I had to be confident and have faith in myself and my horse, regardless of what anyone else said.

We definitely had a long way to go, but after what we had accomplished the previous show season, I had no doubt Jay and I would be number one in the nation and compete in the finals the following September. With 16 points already, I thought we were off to a pretty good start.

The weekend following our return from New York we attended a FHCA show at Rocking Horse Stables in Altoona. We arrived just before noon, set up our trailer, and then waited, and waited, and waited. It had to be the slowest show in history. Although all of Kristine's other students were done by five o'clock, I was just getting started.

Our first class was the Horseshows in the Park Medal. Jay and I had a very nice round, but the judge told the show manager to let me know I should have taken his bell boots off before we went into the ring. As a result, he marked us down because of it. Our second class was a Handy Hunter class. Jay was going very well, but as he came around one of the corners during a rollback he tripped and I heard metal hitting metal. I silently prayed he didn't lose a shoe. He finished the course without any problems and we ended up placing third out of six. As we exited the ring

I leaned over and was relieved to see he still had all his shoes on. Upon closer inspection though, his front right shoe was a bit loose.

At that point we had a decision to make. The fences in the first two classes had been set at 2'6"; for the Marshall and Sterling medal they would be raised to 3'. Normally we would bring Jay over to the schooling area and take him over a few jumps at 3'3" or 3'6". The first time or two over the higher jumps he would usually bump or pull the rail because he was expecting a lower jump, but after that he would be fine. The dilemma was, the schooling area at Rocking Horse was very sandy and deep; if Jay took a bad step he could potentially pull his loose shoe off, making it impossible for us to compete in the medal class. With only three riders entered, if I didn't show, no one would have the opportunity to get points because the class wouldn't fill. I knew Jay would pull a rail if we went into the ring without warming-up, but the worst we could do was third. I chose to skip the schooling and take our chances in the ring.

It was already after seven o'clock by the time they were ready to start the medal, so management offered to let each rider take one jump in the ring at 3' as a warm-up. By doing so, they would avoid losing more time and daylight as the other two riders rode over to the schooling area and back. All three of us agreed. When we took our turn, Jay sent the rail flying just as I had expected. I could only hope it would be enough to remind him to pick up his feet during our class.

We'd gotten to know the show management and crew quite well at the FHCA shows after competing with them for over three years. They were very upset when we lost Chance and were there to witness some of Jay's more impressive moments in the ring. I appreciated the fact that they had always been very supportive of me. One of the show managers, Jeanne, was standing with Kristine and my mom next to the in-gate as I entered the ring. She was kind enough to wish me luck as I passed by and checked to make sure Jay's bell boots were off.

We started off quite well, but halfway through the course Jay pulled one of the rails on an inside jump and stumbled, throwing me off balance. I acted as if nothing happened and encouraged him to continue. We finished without any other problems, but as we walked out of the ring I could hear the loud clanking of his loose shoe.

We ended up finishing third out of three. I was extremely pleased with what had transpired though, and not disappointed at all. The way I looked at it, four points were better than no points. What was even more exciting for me was that Jay had done his job under conditions that were not ideal. He had jumped the entire course without making any attempt to duck out or refuse any obstacle. I told him how proud I was of him as I untacked him at the trailer.

On the way home, my mom surprised me by saying, "Jay really showed a lot of heart out there today. He was trying his best for you even with that loose shoe. If the worst he did under the circumstances was pull a rail; I'm okay with that. I'm beginning to think our old Jay is back."

I responded in agreement. Her comments made me realize we'd accomplished something very important that afternoon; Jay had regained my mother's trust in him.

CHAPTER 14

Our Horse Show Friends

After much discussion, my mom and I decided to bring Jay up to the FHCA show at Canterbury the weekend of October 7th on Saturday morning so he'd only have to spend one night there. When we arrived we were rather surprised to see half the stalls weren't filled. Apparently it was homecoming weekend for the University of Florida and hotel rooms were very hard to come by. I could only hope there would be enough riders to fill my classes.

While we were setting up Jay's stall we ran into one of the riders we'd met while attending shows held at a local farm in the area. Corey was the same age as me and we both felt as though we'd known each other all our lives from the minute we'd met. Her mother, Jyan, was very sweet and a lot of fun. My mom and I truly enjoyed hanging out with them ringside at the shows while we waited for our classes. We were very excited to find out that, like us, they camped at the showgrounds in their RV. Corey showed in the 2'6" Children's Hunter classes, so I got Jay ready early and we headed up to the ring to watch her ride since my classes followed that division.

As always, things never seemed to go as planned. One trainer held up our ring for over an hour while we waited for her to finish coaching a short stirrup rider on the other side of the showgrounds. The rider we were waiting for was in Corey's classes, and even though everyone else in the Children's division had completed their courses, they had to wait for the other trainer to arrive before they could run the flat class. Of course, I couldn't do anything until the Children's division finished. While we waited near the ring with our horses, Corey and I began talking to another rider we'd become familiar with during the past year named Jennifer, or as we called her, Niffer. She normally rode in the same classes I did, so we always seemed to be hanging out together while we waited for our turn to show. Like Corey and me, she was also fifteen. Not surprisingly, the three of us had a great time talking and goofing around for an hour or so before we had to get back to the business of showing.

That first day I only had a 3' schooling class and the Marshall and Sterling medal. I was happy to find out that the medal class filled with three riders, one of which was Niffer. As each of us took our turns in the ring prior to the medal, the other two would cheer us on from the sidelines with Niffer's trainer, Jyan and my mom adding their support. I have to say, my mom and I both felt a real sense of camaraderie with our show friends and had a wonderful time with them that afternoon.

Jay was a bit sticky in the schooling class, but his performance in the medal was phenomenal. I couldn't have been more pleased with him. When we finished our first rounds, the announcer called us back to the ring for a test on the flat. I knew when the voice came over the loudspeaker telling us to drop our stirrups, Jay and I would be hard to beat. Everything was going perfectly until, without warning, the third rider in the class unexpectedly turned right in front of Jay while we were cantering. Her sudden maneuver caused Jay to lose his balance and swap his lead. I immediately realized what had happened and asked for a flying lead change while still riding without stirrups. Although I tried to be as inconspicuous as possible when I asked for the change, there was no way the judge could have missed it because the entire episode had unfolded in the worst possible spot; directly in front her.

I held my breath as I waited in the line-up with the other riders for the results, not knowing what the judge's call would be on the lead swap. I was so thankful when it was announced I had won first place. Niffer took second and an adult rider was third. As I exited the ring I heard some grumbling among a couple of the spectators. They felt the judge must have just decided to ignore the lead change because in their minds it should have counted against me. They assumed she must have really liked me to give me "such a big break." Although Jay did change his lead when he lost his balance, I immediately asked him to fix it. Since it was an equitation class, it was up to the judge to use her discretion to determine if the situation was the result of my poor riding on my part or the actions of my horse, and score me accordingly. In that situation, it really was the fault of the other rider because there had been absolutely no reason for her to turn in front of us and cut across our path.

After untacking Jay and washing him off, I walked him out to the cross country field to meet Corey. We spent about an hour hand grazing our horses and talking. Once it started getting dark, we brought the horses back to the barn to feed them and finish up our barn chores. When I was done, my mom and I took our Papillons, Merrill and Suzu, out for a walk around the barn area. On our way back to the trailer we ran into Corey and Jyan. We spent the next hour and a half talking and sharing horsey stories. As darkness slowly enveloped us, it seemed as though we were the only people left at the showgrounds. Although I'm sure we could have happily talked all night, we eventually decided it was time for us to pack it in and head back to the trailers.

The following day Jay was a bit goofy and started throwing his head during our first equitation class. Then, on the second jump of the outside line, he ran out. In frustration, I proceeded to slap him across the neck in an effort to regain his attention; definitely not the best way to have handled the situation, especially in front of a judge. I finished at the bottom of the placings in both my equitation classes, but was very thankful I wasn't disqualified.

In the medal class Jay attempted to run out again, but I was able to keep him moving forward. It wasn't our prettiest effort and I was thankful we placed second. It was extremely aggravating when he would do his job incredibly well one day and act up the next. I wished I could figure out what was causing it. My best guess was that he didn't like being away from home overnight; then again, it never seemed to bother him the previous year when we spent several days at a time at Fox Lea. It was just another "Jay thing" that would have to be figured out.

As we headed home, my mom and I both agreed we'd probably had more fun that weekend than we'd ever had a horse show. I loved spending time with Corey, Jyan, Niffer and her trainer, and my mom couldn't help but agree. We were really looking forward to the November show so we could spend more time with our friends.

CHAPTER 15

Reengineering Jay

My mom recognized that something drastic had to be done to improve Jay's topline, especially his neck. Over the past year his topline had gradually deteriorated to a point where it looked pretty bad. If we kept going the way we were, no judge at the finals or even the bigger rated shows would even look at us, especially when Jay was being fussy and went into his inverted neck mode. For months I had been working with the bit in an effort to get him round and in frame. We'd finally reached a point where it was obvious what I was doing was not working and he was only getting worse; therefore, my mom decided it was time to ask Vicky if she could help us.

She discussed Jay's issues with her and as she knew she would, Vicky immediately had two solutions to help Jay. First, I would work him under saddle using a running martingale. Secondly, she would let me use her surcingle and neck stretcher to work him on the lunge line.

My mom also mentioned to her that there were a couple of other things we needed to work on and weren't sure what to do. In particular, I had been having trouble getting Jay to perform a smooth turn on the haunches. It had gotten to a point where we would do a combination turn on the forehand haunches; not what we were looking for. We had tried to fix it ourselves, but just couldn't get it to work right. Additionally, as Kristine would always tell me, Jay needed to be lighter on his front end. Not wanting to lose any training time, Vicky made arrangements to come out the following evening to work with Jay and me.

Knowing that when she lunged Jay with the neck stretcher for the first time he'd get pretty worked up, Vicky decided to do the under saddle work first. My mom found a running martingale she'd purchased years ago for one of our other horses in our tack box, and after fitting it to Jay, we were ready to embark on our mission to improve his topline.

Once we were in the ring, Vicky had me walk Jay around to get the feel of the martingale's pressure. He was definitely not a happy camper when he realized he'd have to keep his head and neck in the proper position. My mom commented later that as we worked through the posting trot, sitting trot, and canter, she was astounded by how beautifully Jay was moving again! He was engaging his back end and actually stepping out. The short strides he liked to take disappeared. It was a lot of work for me because he still tried to fight it and invert his neck, but my mom could see that the form and movement we needed were definitely still there. She was almost jumping up and down in her excitement. Vicky seemed rather amused by my mom's reaction. It was almost too easy, especially after all the months I'd spent trying to get Jay to do it myself without any type of aids.

One important bit information Vicky shared with me during our training session that really hit home was that the trainers we see at shows don't necessarily ride the horses every day to make them look so good. What they know how to do is use the appropriate training tools to get the results they needed. She instantly made a believer out of me.

The next step was teaching me how to smoothly perform the turn on the haunches. Since Jay sometimes seemed confused about what I was asking him to do, Vicky told me to decide what cue I was going to use based on how he normally responded and then use it consistently. After he attempted to repeatedly turn on the forehand or sidepass, Vicky stood next to Jay and pressed on his shoulder to help me understand how to make him move his front end. Then she explained to me that a lot of riders get confused because they think the turn on the haunches is performed from a standstill. She told me to always remember that you have to have forward movement to do it correctly. In about fifteen minutes, we had it down.

One of the other issues we'd continually had with Jay during the past year was an inability to get him to lighten up on his front end. Of course, Vicky had a solution for that as well. She instructed me to trot along the arena from one light post to the other. Every time we were even with the post, I would stop Jay and take two or three steps backwards. I would then walk forward, turn on the haunches and do the same thing in the opposite direction to the other post. She said even though it was a training method used for reining horses, it would definitely help Jay.

It was an exercise that would prove to be very enlightening for us. After several passes, Vicky pointed out that unlike most horses, Jay stopped with his front end rather than sitting back on his hind end. As such, the goal would be to eventually get him to anticipate the halt and backward steps so that he'd shift his weight back. We continued the exercise at the trot and canter until he became a little fussy and then moved on to other things.

After some additional flat work and a bit more of the stop, back, reverse exercise, Vicky was ready to introduce Jay to the neck stretcher. It was essentially a bungee cord that ran from either side of the surcingle up along each side of his bridle and over his poll. After nearly twenty minutes of overly dramatic moments from Jay as he acclimated himself to the neck stretcher, he finally began to relax and carry himself in the proper position at the walk and trot. For me, it was an amazing display to watch; Jay was a horse transformed! Vicky pointed out that the results she was getting on the lunge line were the same ones I'd achieved under saddle. It was a definite "wow" moment for me because I hadn't been able to see him when I was riding.

By the time the training session ended, the three of us could barely contain our excitement at the prospect of transforming Jay. Although we only had a couple of days to practice our new exercises before our next show, we were eager to see how much improvement we'd gain in a short period of time. Considering how far I'd come with him already, once we had him moving correctly again, I felt we could certainly be contenders at any finals. The future was looking quite bright.

CHAPTER 16

Affirmation of My Riding Skills

Earlier in the year we'd attended some shows at Full Partners Farm, a private boarding and training facility in Newberry. At first, my mom and I both felt a bit awkward because we were the only "outsiders" in attendance; all of the other competitors were students, boarders or interns at the farm. We certainly seemed to attract a lot of attention those first couple of shows as everyone wondered who the "strangers" were. Of course, Corey and Jyan were very friendly from day one, and in time the rest of the people there got to know us and made us feel very welcome.

After attending several of their shows, I'd come to look forward to the challenges of the unusual jumping obstacles, rails and objects they placed in their ring. Since Jay and I never had a chance to school in the ring before our classes like the competitors who rode there, those shows became a true test of our skill and determination. Naturally, the more challenging jumps were only included in the medal course, so we usually didn't even have a chance to jump them during our warm-up rounds.

Our first interesting jump situation had occurred the previous July when an obstacle was included in the medal course that consisted of two bright blue barrels turned over on their sides at the base of a jump. After Jay ran out on our first attempt, I realized I was going to have to ensure we were as prepared as possible for anything we could encounter there in the future. At their next show we faced bouquets of plastic flowers strewn several yards in front of a jump and oddly shaped split rail cypress poles. Somehow, even though our warm-up rounds were ugly, in each case we managed to pull it together to do well in the medal round.

The October 14th show proved to be no different. The jump that had barrels in front of it several months earlier was set up as an oxer with a blue tarp attached to some two by four's underneath it to simulate a water jump. My mom had been talking about making a similar jump to use at home for the last year or so, but never got around to making it.

As expected, the only course that included the faux liverpool was the medal.

My mom knew she had to come up with something quick for Jay to school over that would look similar in appearance, in order to keep him from refusing or running out. While she looked around for objects she could set up for us to jump in the warm-up ring, she asked me to start schooling Jay on the flat with the running martingale to see how he'd react to it away from home. I was quite happy when he immediately settled right in to work and kept himself in frame.

Looking around the ring my mom discovered several jump planks that were painted with blue and white stripes. They didn't look exactly the same as the tarp, but she thought she could create a similar effect by placing them flat under an oxer. Once the practice jump was set up I took Jay over it several times without incident at 3'. She then raised it to 3'6", fully expecting him to pull the rail the first time, but he cleared it easily. Still not convinced that he'd go over the tarp, she decided I needed a little insurance. The only objects in the ring that were the same color as the tarp were the plastic barrels that had been used in the show several months before. She rolled two of them over and placed them under the oxer between the rails. She hoped, in Jay's mind, they would be more intimidating than the tarp. Again and again he went over the jump easily without hesitation; we were ready.

The show ring they used at the time was quite unique. It was built around several large oak trees in an effort to provide riders with shade during the summer, which in itself was a great idea. The downside was there were exposed tree roots in some areas and on one side of the ring there was extremely limited clearance between one of the trees and the perimeter fence. Additionally, there were large rocks in several areas that had to be maneuvered around. The footing was sand based and bit deep at both ends. Another interesting aspect of the ring was that it was built on an incline, which presented its own problems for riders and horses. If you didn't have enough horse going up the hill through the deep sand, you couldn't get the correct number of strides in the line. Conversely, if you rode too fast down the hill, you could leave strides out or chip in.

In my first warm-up of the day I ran into the going too fast down the hill problem. Because of the trees in the ring, there weren't many options available for setting up courses. Inevitably, there would always be one inside jump set up between two trees in the center of the ring that could be jumped alone or as an obstacle in a bending line. For the first course, it was set up as the first jump of a tight bending line coming diagonally down the hill. Jay jumped it beautifully, but I forgot to bring him back afterward so he had quite a bit of forward momentum coming out of it. By the time I realized I had miscalculated, he was headed straight for the standard of the second jump. I was way too late when I tried to turn him toward the jump pole and he came to a full and complete stop facing the standard. At first I thought I'd be able to stay on when he slammed on the brakes, but I was too far forward and ended up landing on my side directly in front of him. Realizing what a precarious position I was in, I quickly rolled out of the way. Once I moved, Jay calmly walked to the other side of the ring. I brushed myself off, walked over to him and hopped back on. My mom called out to me to let me know the show manager said I could redo the line before exiting the ring. The second time was perfect.

She told me later that while she hadn't wanted to make a big deal about it at the time, when I fell off Jay and landed in front of him she had been absolutely terrified. Had he taken one step forward he would have stepped on my body as I lay across the ground just inches from his front legs. It was quite some time before her heart stopped pounding and her hands stopped shaking. She was extremely thankful that he'd composed himself the way he had.

Several riders later I went back in for my second round, which rode beautifully. Jay did his part and cleared everything easily and with style. The judge asked whether or not we were being judged for a hunter round. When we told her it was just another warm-up, she said it was too bad because she'd placed us second out of six.

The medal class was next and I was more than happy to let the other riders go first. One adult rider was eliminated after falling off. Another adult rider had a really good round, but her horse took the water jump as if it were six feet high. The next rider was about my age and she had difficulty when her horse refused that same jump the first time they approached. The final rider before me had some difficultly with the inside jump between the trees which caused her horse to pull the rail coming down the hill. The door was definitely open.

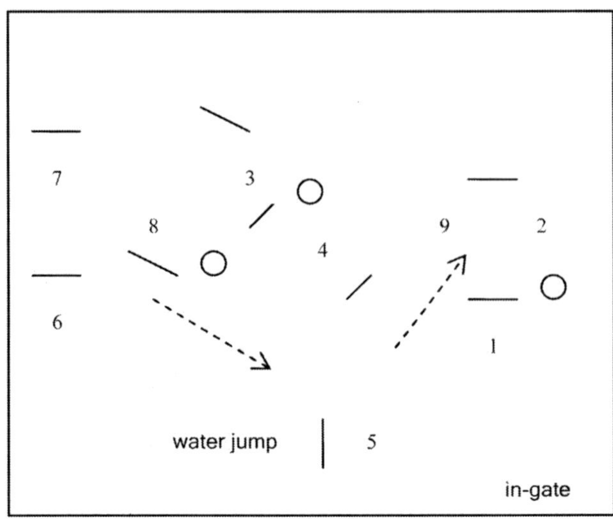

Marshall and Sterling Children's Horse Medal

Jay jumped amazingly well and had no problems with the water jump. Then at the end of the course I surprised everyone, including my mom, with a tight turn that was completely unexpected. All the other riders finished their course by going around the water jump at the end of the ring and taking an outside track around jump one to the second jump in the line. I rolled tightly back in front the water jump and took the inside track past jump one, which set us up perfectly for the second jump of the outside line. Unfortunately, Jay was a bit off balance going into the last jump after he lost his footing in the sand going up the hill. He cleared it without incident, but it wasn't his prettiest effort. When I came out of the ring my mom told me she had to give me credit; I took a risk and attempted something no one else even thought to try.

After a short work off on the flat, I was awarded first place. The adult was second and the other two girls were third and fourth. I told my mom later I was glad I went last because I didn't want anyone to see me try the tight turn before they rode. She chuckled and said admiringly, "That's my girl; thinking about the course and making her plan."

All in all I was very proud of Jay's behavior. It was at that point I came to the realization that he really preferred it when I took charge and guided him through the course; something that was the complete opposite of what I had experienced with Ticky and Chance. In addition, although the footing made it difficult for him to canter around the ring at a smooth pace, it did seem as though he was generally moving better during our courses and his jumps were more consistent. And best of all, even after I fell off, he kept his composure and willingly continued to work with me. We were definitely making progress.

In the weeks that followed we attended several more one day shows. Jay and I did very well in all of them and our point total continued to mount. There was one show in particular that really stood out for me, the November Full Partners show. I was admittedly a bit disappointed when I arrived and noticed there were no water jumps or jumps with rustic poles on the course. The only potentially "spooky" jump was one that had four blue barrels set down on their sides in front of the rail to simulate a roll top. Looking at the courses, I knew Jay wouldn't have any problems.

After I schooled him, we headed over to the ring for the start of our classes. Happily, Jay and I were both extremely relaxed as we entered the ring for our first warm-up. Other than chipping in to the first jump of the outside line going uphill, our round was very quiet, smooth and controlled. The second course was just about perfect. We were finding all our distances, getting the proper number of strides, and rating throughout the course to manage the "hilly" terrain.

I was the last to go out of five teenaged girls in the medal. Each round we'd ridden had been better than the one before and our medal round was the best yet. When we came out of the ring, my mom quickly removed Jay's martingale for the test on the flat. Jay and I were definitely "on" and I couldn't help but smile when the judge told us to drop our stirrups. After finishing the test, we lined up in the center of the ring and I was announced as the winner. I was so excited I didn't pay attention to how the other riders placed.

As I exited, my mom laughingly said "I guess you want me to get your ribbon for you."

I smiled broadly and eagerly nodded my head.

Most of the riders and spectators had already left the ring area since the medal was the last class. The box of ribbons had been moved to the show office booth, so my mom made her way over to it to collect my ribbon. As I waited with Corey and Jyan for my mom to return with my prize, I was quite surprised when the judge approached me. She complimented me on my riding and told me I had been so far ahead of the other riders after the over fence portion, she didn't need to watch me on the flat because I'd already won the class. I thanked her for sharing her feedback with me and told her I really appreciated it.

With ribbon in hand, we all made our way in the direction of the entrance gate. While my mom held it open to let Jay and me pass, the judge asked her if we just trailered in for the medal. She told her we did and explained that I was trying to accumulate points for a year-end award. The judge responded by saying she had been disappointed I didn't do some of the other classes because she would have liked to have seen more of Jay and me. We both thanked her again for sharing her comments with us. It was a wonderful way to end the day!

CHAPTER 17

Overcoming the Past

The November FHCA show at Canterbury was the last one of the 2006 season and the year-end awards were scheduled to be presented on Sunday. To make the final day more competitive, show management had double pointed all the classes. Throughout the year I had focused on both the Marshall and Sterling medal and the Junior/Adult Amateur Equitation division for that circuit. Going into the competition, I was leading the Jr/AA division by nine points. Based on my mom's calculations, the only way I could drop to second place was if the rider currently holding that position, my friend Niffer, won both the over fence and flat classes and I placed lower than second in both. I knew my adrenaline would be pumping all weekend the minute she told me it could come down to the last class.

Any riders who placed in the Marshall and Sterling or Horseshows in the Park medals throughout the year qualified for a year-end medal final on Saturday night. The evening's festivities would also include a best dressed dog contest, a mini-medals final, and a hunter final. I wanted to participate in the medal final, if for no other reason than to school Jay. I thought back to the finals show the previous January when he had spooked at just about everything and hadn't listened to me. My main goal was to get him through the course without incident. It was the first opportunity we'd had in nearly a year to show in a covered arena at night and I hoped we'd have a completely different outcome.

Kristine had told us the previous week that she would be attending the show with some of her other students. She wouldn't be there specifically for me, but would help out if I needed her. To prepare me for the final, my mom asked her to come over to the house the night before we left for the show to work with me on a couple of things she felt I needed to "pretty" up. We spent time working on smoothing out backing, simple lead changes and the counter canter. Since FHCA sometimes included tests in the first round of their medal courses, we also practiced one we'd seen several times; canter a jump, halt, reverse, and trot the next jump.

On Saturday I was scheduled for a warm-up class and the Marshall and Sterling medal. Jay went over everything without issue in the schooling round. For the medal class, there were only four riders including Niffer and me. No one wanted to go first, so I volunteered. The in-course test was the exact one I had practiced the night before at home. Jay went around the course quietly and calmly, but when the time came to halt at a cone, I misjudged the distance and overshot it. My strategy had been to stop from the canter with minimal trotting, but it didn't work out quite as I had planned. We backed the five steps smoothly, reversed, trotted the next fence, and continued the course. At the end Jay completed a lovely tight rollback on the inside of a jump to the final single. Other than the one mistake, it was a pretty good round and I placed second behind Niffer.

The medal was the last regularly scheduled class of the day. Upon its conclusion, management advised everyone that they would be removing some jumps from the ring and anyone participating in the finals that evening could take one schooling round to practice. They were starting with the higher fences first, so Niffer, Corey and I were able to complete our rounds early, which allowed us to take a bit of a break before the nighttime festivities began.

While walking back to the barn, we ran into Kristine. She told us she was too tired to stay for the finals and after schooling a couple of her other riders for their practice rounds, she would be heading back to her hotel for the night. I was admittedly rather disappointed that she'd decided not to stay to watch me ride since it was the first medal final of any kind I'd ever competed in. But I had to remind myself, she wasn't there to coach me, she was there with her other students.

Prior to the event, show management had sent out info on the various finals competitions, including a Best Dressed Barn Dog class to start the evening off. When my mom had heard about the contest, she immediately knew she had to come up with something for Merrill and Suzu to wear. Much to Merrill's humiliation, she made him a Captain Jack Sparrow costume complete with wig and beard. For Suzu she made a lovely dress, hat, and wig for her debut as Elizabeth Swann. Everyone at the show absolutely loved their costumes! Our biggest challenge of the evening was getting them to keep their wigs on for the judging in the covered arena. Even though they weren't chosen as the winners, they were definitely the crowd favorites.

The mini-medal final ran after the dog contest, so I had time to tack Jay up and watch some of the younger riders before my class. After nearly an hour of competition, it was time for the HSITP Medal Final to begin. Nearly twenty riders were scheduled to compete and I was eighth in the order. As we watched the other riders go, I noticed that they were all riding it like a hunter course; using the entire ring and making wide, sweeping turns. To me, it was an opportunity to show my control and "wow" the panel of three judges. The first jump was an inside single facing the in-gate at the opposite end of the arena. Since all of the previous riders had entered the ring and completed a courtesy circle before approaching the jump, I decided to sit trot into the ring, pick up the canter and ride directly to the jump.

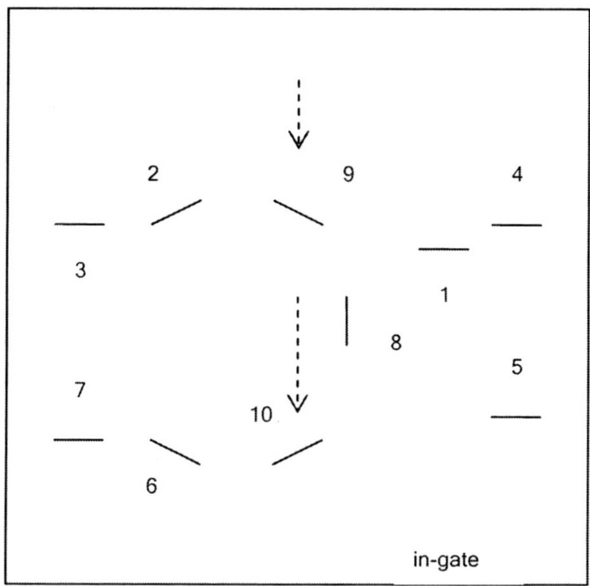

2006 FHCA Horseshows in the Park Medal Finals
Round 1

Unlike the debacle the previous January, it was quickly apparent that Jay was listening to me as I guided him around the course. While many of the riders had to pull and yank their horses into the rollback to jump three, I just turned my head and Jay followed my lead. We took the next jumps easily and quietly. The last two were set in the center of the ring, angled opposite each other. All of the riders were going straight into the first jump from the far corner and bending back to the second. I, on the other hand, turned to the first jump from the center of the ring on the far side, jumped it at an angle, then rode to the second jump in a straight line and took it at an angle. My mom said some of the trainers milling around the in-gate were quite impressed. It was one of those moments when it felt like Jay and I were completely in sync with each other; it was incredible!

Four of us were called back to test, and going into it, I held first place. Niffer was behind me in second, an adult rider was third and another girl was fourth. We were told to line up in the corner facing the stands near jump seven. Once we were all in place the announcer gave us our test; go directly to fence eight in the opposite direction from the first round, continue to fences two and three, halt, and counter canter back to the line between jumps two and three.

The first rider was confused and unsure of the instructions, although she managed to complete all of the requirements except the counter canter. The adult performed the test exceptionally well and Niffer's was also very good. My ride was going great until the flat stage. The other riders all turned the corner after the rollback to set themselves up for the counter canter back. I got myself hung up when I executed a lovely halt straight off the jump thinking that it would show my control. I miscalculated though because then I had to pick up the counter canter and turn completely around. Instead, I did a turn on the haunches and was trying so hard to pick up the counter canter that I allowed Jay to take several trot steps before doing so.

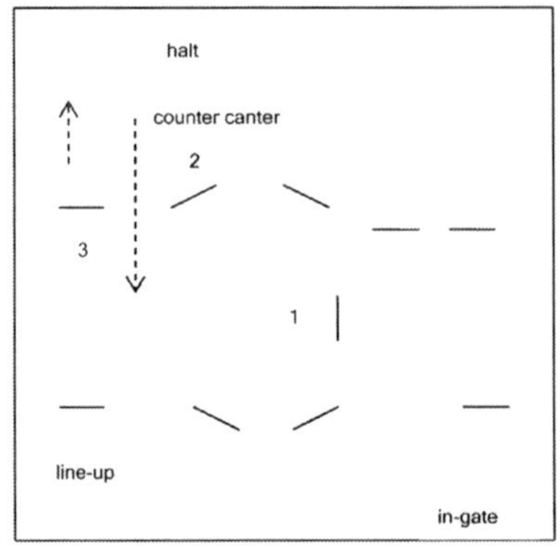

2006 FHCA Horseshows in the Park Medal Finals
Round 2

Thankfully, even with the stride break, our solid first round kept us in second place with the Reserve Championship behind the adult. For our efforts we received a lovely ribbon and silver cup trophy. For me, the most exciting part of the entire night was the victory gallop around the arena. It was something I had always wanted to do and Jay and I were in our glory! I felt bad Kristine wasn't there to share the experience with us. Nevertheless, I thoroughly enjoyed every minute of it.

The next day I started with a warm-up even though the jump set-up from the previous night hadn't changed. The classes were double in size, so I knew I'd really have to stand out. The Junior/Amateur Adult Equitation Over Fences class was next. I wanted to go in toward the end so I let about six riders go before me. All but one of them rode the course very conservatively. While reviewing the course I noticed there was really only one spot where I could do something more difficult. About midway through the course I had to jump the second jump of the outside line coming down on the right, come back around to a jump in the middle of the ring set on the right side parallel to the rail and then come around the far end of the arena to the inside line coming down from the left corner into a rollback. Most of the riders rode all the way around the end of the ring off the outside line and then around the first jump of the opposite outside line so they could get into the parallel jump straight. Then they rode straight to the rail before they turned.

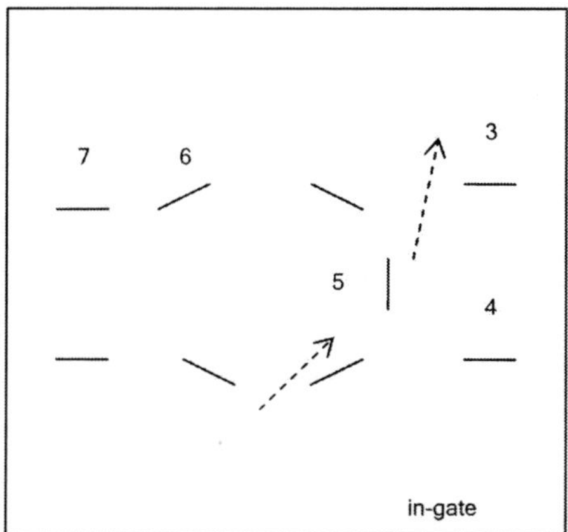

2006 FHCA Horseshows in the Park Finals
Junior/Adult Amateur Equitation Over Fences

I decided that I would take it to the next level. My idea was to come off the outside line, go between the two jumps of the inside lines, take the parallel jump at an angle, and then turn in front of the outside jump. The only problem was it would require an extremely tight rollback to get between the jumps. At the angle I would be approaching, I could potentially get myself hung up going into the parallel jump. When I asked my mom what she thought, she told me it would be tough, but if I felt comfortable doing it I should go for it. The most important thing was for me to know my plan and execute it to the best of my ability. She admitted later that it was one of the few times she had doubts that I could pull it off.

As I came off the outside line, I overshot the rollback between the inside jumps slightly and had to make a bit of an exaggerated turn back. I took the parallel jump at a very sharp angle and was thrilled Jay didn't even hesitate. Off the jump we barely had to turn and went straight to the end of the ring on the quarter line. It was just like the night before, quiet and efficient. I think a lot of people watching were shocked by what we had pulled off. Niffer's trainer even complimented me when I came out of the ring. The judge seemed to appreciate my effort and awarded me first place.

Then I entered the ring with seven other riders for the flat class. Jay was going around perfectly and for some reason decided to throw in a lead change as we came down the quarter line on his right lead. Before he could even take two strides I asked him to change it back. I hoped the judge could see that it wasn't the result of anything I did; we were coming straight down the line and I hadn't even moved. I was quite relieved when they announced that I had placed third. As I exited the ring, my mom excitedly told me I had clinched the year-end Grand Championship for the Junior/Amateur Adult Equitation division. I was ecstatic!

After completing our equitation classes, Jay and I waited by the side of the ring to watch Niffer's hunter rounds and wait for the medal class. While I watched some of the other riders complete their courses, I zoned out and didn't see her as she made her way over toward me from behind. As she approached Jay's left flank, she suddenly leaned over and popped me on the back of my helmet with her riding crop; it was something we were fond of doing to each other while we waited for our classes.

Normally, after she popped me, I'd just pop her back. Unfortunately, there was a completely different and unexpected outcome. Of course, had I been sitting on my horse properly that probably wouldn't have been the case. As it was, I had my left leg across the front of the saddle, almost as if I was sitting sidesaddle. My mom had told me time and time again not to sit like that, but naturally I never thought anything would happen; that day I quickly found out how wrong I was.

Since I didn't see Niffer coming and wasn't expecting it, my entire body jumped with the impact. My startled reaction caused Jay to spook and I ended up falling off his right side. As I went down, my left leg tangled in the reins. For a few moments I hobbled on one foot attempting to untangle my leg while Jay backed away from me in a panic. I eventually freed myself, lost my balance and landed on my butt. I somehow managed to hold on to the reins and was quickly able to get him under control.

Luckily, no one was hurt. Of course, all of the trainers, parents and show staff standing nearby glared at Niffer as if she had committed some heinous crime. No, she probably shouldn't have done it; but Niffer, Corey and I had done the same thing to each other many times in the past without incident and thought nothing of it. Poor Niffer was devastated, completely blaming herself for causing me to fall off. She immediately began apologizing profusely on the verge of tears. My mom and I told her not to worry; it was an accident and a good lesson for the both of us.

There were a few riders showing in the HSITP medal so it gave me a chance to get myself together before the Marshall and Sterling medal started. Since it was the same course for both classes, I also had the opportunity to watch how it rode. It was a relatively easy course with the same rollback at the far end that we'd executed at least five times in the last two days. When I entered the ring everything started off beautifully, but as I turned back to take the second jump of the rollback, Jay turned his head slightly about two strides out to look at the extra jumps that were stored outside the ring. Although he was on the verge of spooking, I absolutely refused to let him do so and made him move forward to the jump. Unfortunately, he was off balance and pulled the rail as we went over. When it fell, it pulled down the gate beneath it. The result was very loud and very ugly. All I could do was continue through the course unflustered and act as though nothing had happened. With the exception of the downed rail, my mom said it was another great round for us.

As my mom expected, I was quite disappointed when I came out of the ring. She told me there was nothing I could have done differently; it was just something Jay decided to throw at me. For whatever reason, a lot of horses had been spooky along that same side all day. As far as I was concerned though, Jay had no excuses.

Seven of the eight riders finished the course. Of those, one other rider also pulled a rail and another had a refusal; we hoped for a fifth or sixth place finish at best. We decided to wait by the ring to see how the other riders placed so my mom could figure out how the points would be affected.

We were both stunned when I was the first one called back to test. After my name was announced and I re-entered the ring, I could hear some grumbling around the in-gate. Most of it was coming from the family of another girl who had completed the course without pulling a rail. I was extremely appreciative the judge seemed to understand that the downed rail was not the result of anything I had done, just like the lead swap earlier. My guess was that the people grumbling didn't understand the judging criteria for equitation.

Two other teenaged girls were called back in second and third respectively, and another rider I'd competed against at other shows, Michael, was in first. We were told to line up at the far end of the ring near the announcer's booth keeping our backs to the ring during the test. We were then given our instructions; counter canter to the second jump of the outside line in front of the judge, canter the first fence of the opposite outside line, halt and sit trot back to the line. I was the first to go and knew as I rode it, our test was absolutely flawless!

My mom told me afterward that the horse of the girl in third place had gotten pretty fast around the corner after the first jump, which made her halt a bit rough. The girl in second place started off well, but she was riding too far forward. After the second jump, her position caused the horse to land off balance, pull the rail and nearly fall to his knees. Michael's test was very good and she knew he would hold on to first. Her guess was the girl who was second going into the test would drop to fourth and both the girl in third place and I would each move up one place.

When the results were announced they created quite a commotion. Michael finished first and I was second. My mom was a bit surprised that quite a few of the other trainers and parents were extremely upset by the judge's decision. Yet only one trainer even approached us about it because she knew that I usually only showed in equitation classes. Since her experience was mainly in other disciplines, she didn't understand how I could have placed higher with a pulled rail than some of the other riders who had kept all the rails up. My mom explained that in equitation the judge, at their discretion, determines whether to fault the horse or rider for a downed rail. She told her it's probably also the reason I finished higher than some in the flat class even when Jay swapped his lead down the line. Apparently the judge realized in both cases that Jay was at fault, not me. In the end, I was quite pleased with the way it turned out. Jay had redeemed himself, and came through for me when it really mattered. My mom and I were very thankful the judge acknowledged my riding abilities and had rewarded me accordingly.

While we waited for the points to be tabulated for the year-end awards, I untacked and washed Jay, then started packing up the trailer. Finally, after waiting patiently for what seemed like hours it was official; I was the 2006 Junior/Adult Amateur Equitation Grand Champion! For my efforts I received a huge championship ribbon and a large silver bowl mounted on a wooden base. In addition, I was surprised to find out that Jay had finished third in the Regular Working Hunter division.

As we walked from the office back to the barn, my mom told she was very proud of me and what I'd accomplished during the past year. Even when it seemed as if everything was working against me and the odds were insurmountable, I'd refused to quit. It was a true test of my willpower that I wouldn't let my horse quit either. In less than a year, with lots of hard work, I had turned him into a pretty darn good equitation mount. She said she didn't know many kids my age that could have brought Jay to that point without a trainer actually schooling the horse for them on a regular basis. Yes, Kristine, Vicky and my mom were there along the way to guide and work with me, but I was the one who had to make it happen. It made me so happy when she said I was "a truly amazing kid!"

We were pleased to find out that Corey and Niffer had also done well in the year-end standings. Corey finished the year as the Grand

Champion in the Children's Hunter and Equitation divisions, and Niffer was the Reserve Champion in the Junior/Amateur Adult Hunter and Equitation divisions. All three of us had worked very hard throughout the year and I was glad we all ended up doing so well.

CHAPTER 18

Salvation for Jay's Hooves

For whatever reason, since the previous summer Jay had been doing a wonderful job for me in the show ring and we were all very pleased. He was calm and quiet for the most part, but there were several things going on that we needed to get a handle on. If we could just get him to stop periodically adding half strides in front of jumps and use his body better going over obstacles, he would be awesome. Kristine just wrote his form and jumping style off to him "being Jay;" yet I wasn't convinced.

The other thing I wished he would stop was running away when I tried to catch him in the pasture. It was something he had just started doing over the summer and it was extremely annoying. We ended up wasting a lot of time playing the chase and corner game whenever I wanted to ride. Another aspect of Jay that was perplexing me was how he could perform beautifully at a one day show or even the first day of a weekend show, but the second day was always a bit rough because he'd start doing weird "Jay things." Something wasn't right, but I couldn't put my finger on it. Worst of all, neither could my mom.

By October my mom had grown decidedly uncomfortable with Ron. She didn't feel he was doing that great a job on the boys' feet; he was okay, but he certainly wasn't even close to being in the same league as Haws or our former farrier. When Jay had been repeatedly pulling his front shoes, Ron's solution had been to change his front shoes to ones with clips. My mom specifically asked him if they were wedges and he advised her that they were the exact same shoes Haws had put on him. Although she seemed to remember Haws mentioning something about having to make clips himself for aluminum wedge shoes because they didn't sell them that way, she took the farrier at his word. She would later regret she didn't check them herself.

It was just before Christmas when she finally reached her limit with him. A few of weeks after Ron's visit in November, my mom noticed that Riley's hooves were breaking off the sides in chunks, which caused her great concern. Jay's left rear ankle had been puffy for months and his back hooves looked like they had bubbles in front and on the sides. When she had mentioned the swelling to Ron a few months back, he said it the result of Jay stepping on himself. What really irked her was that our horses were on a six week trimming schedule that we had always followed religiously; therefore, there was no excuse for their feet to look they way they did. And to top it off, Bo's and Cheyenne's weren't in much better condition. My mom had already talked to Vicky about using her farrier, and with the horses' hooves looking so bad, she finally decided she was done with Ron.

On New Year's Eve morning we met Vicky's farrier, Joe and his brother, George, for the first time. When he arrived, my mom pulled Riley up for him first since she had talked to him about putting shoes on his front feet when they had spoken on the phone. He was genuinely shocked by the condition of Riley's feet and was surprised to hear that he had been trimmed six weeks earlier. He trimmed him up as best he could, but shoes weren't going to be an option for a while because his hoof walls on the side were so broken up. In addition, Riley's toes were much too long, which explained why he had a tendency to drag his back feet. He also mentioned that Riley's frogs hadn't been trimmed well and were contracted. To make matters worse, he had some thrush underneath the frogs that needed to be treated. After spending an hour trimming Riley, Joe moved on to Jay.

As he lifted Jay's front feet to pull off the shoes, my mom noticed that they weren't wedges. She was stunned! She had specifically told Ron that Jay needed to be in wedges until his heels grew back. She never thought to check, and since I groom my horse, my mom never looked at his shoes. While that was bad enough, his shoes were so far forward, the backs of his feet were hanging over the edge and his heels were non-existent. He was actually worse than he had been when Ron started working on him nearly nine months before!

Joe explained that Jay's toes were also much too long and the angles way off. He showed us how the shoe should have been placed farther back on his hoof to protect the entire foot. His back feet were in pretty much the same condition; toes too long, bad angles and shoes too far forward. When Joe asked about the swelling in Jay's left hind foot, we told him Ron had said it was because he stepped on himself. Joe disagreed and explained that his hoof wasn't properly balanced which was causing it to grow sideways. By that point my mom was absolutely furious! She said she could only blame herself; something told her not to trust Ron, but she hadn't listened.

Joe advised us that it would take a couple of trims to get Jay close to where he needed to be. He was concerned he wouldn't be able to keep the front shoes on for six weeks since the sides of his hooves were so broken up and thin. Plus, he could only place two nails on each side because his toes had to be taken back so far. Jay's frogs were also contracted and he had thrush underneath. When he was finished, Joe mentioned that Jay might be a bit sore from all the work he'd done and it would be best if we let him stay out 24/7 for a couple of days. He said normally he would recommend that a horse with issues like Jay's not be worked for six months to a year, but he understood our situation and would do everything in his power to get and keep Jay sound.

After spending almost two hours on Jay, Joe moved to Cheyenne and Bo. Not surprisingly, they both had contracted frogs and thrush. Poor Bo had extensive thrush under his frogs because they hadn't been trimmed properly in months. In all the years we'd owned horses we'd never had a problem with thrush, particularly since our pasture is high and dry sand.

Joe was exceptionally thorough in his work; he measured each angle and heel to ensure the hoof was level. In all, it took over four and a half hours for him to take care of the boys. Interestingly, Ron never once measured any of the horses' feet and was usually done with all of them in two hours or less. The only other farrier I'd ever met that was so diligent in his work was Haws. I could only hope that Joe would prove to be as conscientious going forward.

We gave both Riley and Jay a few days off to adjust to their new trims. As soon as I began riding them, the difference in their movement was quite noticeable. Riley wasn't dragging his back feet and was moving beautifully, but the changes in Jay were unbelievable. He was getting a lot more extension in the front and breaking better in the back, just like he used to when I first got him. Over the jumps he was getting more bascule and not hollowing his back. And best of all, when I asked him to take the long distance, he didn't hesitate or throw in a half stride. Yet the most telling of all the changes was that he no longer ran away from me when I went out to the pasture to pull him up.

He had been trying to tell us something was wrong, but we hadn't listened. Instead of the psycho crazy horse he'd become last winter when the first new farrier messed up his feet, his messages had been much more subtle and we'd missed them. My mom and I felt so guilty. Thankfully, we made the change to Joe before any of the horses reached a point where they sustained permanent damage.

The timing of the transition to Joe actually ended up being ideal. Due to the outbreak of neurological equine herpesvirus, most of the horse shows in Florida from late-December through February were cancelled. The down time gave Jay a chance to adjust to his new trim and ease the strain on his leg muscles. When I realized how much stress the improper hoof trimming had been putting on his legs, I was amazed Jay had been willing to jump at all. I finally understood why he would add strides, jump weird and be difficult the second day of a show; his legs were sore. I knew it would take time to get his hooves to grow back properly, but I fervently hoped the changes would turn Jay back into the beautifully jumping horse he had been the year before when he had won multiple hunter championships.

Poor Joe probably had no idea when he came out that first day how much time he would end up spending at our house working on Jay's hooves in the coming months. Inevitably, Jay would pull a shoe at the worst possible time, usually right before a show, and Joe would have to make a special trip out to fix it. I really appreciated how he would make time in his schedule to come out and work his farrier magic, even when we called him at the last minute. It didn't matter if it was at night or on a weekend; he was always there when we needed him. And each time he came out for a shoe emergency he was patient and understanding, explaining that it wasn't Jay's fault he'd lost a shoe; the problems he was having were the result of the damage that had been done to his hoof walls by the irregular growth and poor trimming. Not to worry though, in time everything would grow back normally. In the interim, all we had to do was call him if there was a problem and he'd be there for us.

CHAPTER 19

Number One in the Nation

On Friday, January 26th the Marshall and Sterling points were updated on the website and I was in first place with 74 points! All I had to do was stay there. I was still missing 20 points from two shows, but was well ahead of the second place rider from New Jersey who had 44 points. I knew the farther along we went, the more competitive it would become; but that's what was it was all about. I planned to accumulate as many points as possible by August as my options for showing were rather limited in the summer, unlike the kids up North. Of course, someone could always come out of nowhere like I did the previous year, but I was confident that wouldn't be an issue as long as Jay could keep his shoes on.

The January FHCA show had to be cancelled due to the herpesvirus outbreak. At the January Barrington Hill show Jay threw a shoe right before the medal class and we had to scratch. As a result, we didn't have a chance to compete in any medal classes from mid-December until early March. Fortunately, at the beginning of the year we discovered that some local show circuits had added the Marshall and Sterling classes to their schedules, which would allow me to make up for lost time. Since the local shows were generally less expensive than the rated ones, they would provide more economical opportunities for me to accrue points. Between school, extracurricular activities and shows, I knew I was going to be very busy in the coming months.

We found out in mid-February that a USHJA clinic hosted by Don Stewart was scheduled on Friday evening, March 2nd at the HITS showgrounds in Ocala. The purpose of the clinic was for Don to provide his insight as a trainer and judge while reviewing some of the rides from the 2004 Washington Medal Finals. My mom thought it would be a great opportunity for us to learn what judges were looking for in equitation. When we mentioned it to Corey and Jyan they also agreed it would be beneficial to hear his perspective on the subject. We made plans to meet them at the showgrounds, so we could all attend together.

When the evening of the event finally arrived, we began to think we weren't going to make it. Between huge brush fires along the Florida Turnpike near our house and torrential rains up in Ocala, the normally uneventful hour and a half drive to the showgrounds took well over two and a half hours. My mom called Jyan about a half hour before the clinic was scheduled to start to find out where they were. She let us know they'd just arrived at showgrounds and were heading for the concession tent where the event was being held. My mom told her we were about ten minutes away and asked her to hold seats for us. Thankfully the rain let up a bit by the time we arrived, but the grounds were completely saturated. We slogged through the mud, umbrella in hand, attempting to avoid the worst spots.

Several televisions had been set up on one side of the tent and upon entering we immediately saw Jyan and Corey at a table in the back. While we waited for Don to begin, we had a chance to catch up since we hadn't seen them for several months. They let us know that, as of December, Corey had moved up to 3' and was planning on trying to qualify for the Marshall and Sterling Children's Medal Finals. I was thrilled because if she did qualify I'd have a friend to hang out with up in New York!

As Don reviewed the selected rides from the finals, he explained how he would have scored the round as compared to the scores given by the actual judges. While he did agree with some of the scores, the variances between his score and even those among the judges themselves, was often significant. Watching the video, I was rather surprised at some of the high scores received by riders with weak legs and poor position. He proceeded to share his viewpoint that there needed to be some type of standardization in the scoring for equitation to alleviate the sometimes large discrepancies between judges. It was very interesting to hear his perspective, and his insight into the world of junior equitation was a truly eye opening experience.

At the conclusion, we quickly made our way back to the cars through the giant mud bog. We wished Jyan and Corey a safe trip and told them we'd see them in the morning at the Sawgrass Horse Show Association competition.

The following morning started off gloomy and rainy. On the trip up to Newberry we hit pockets of rain, some of which were pretty heavy. I was afraid they might cancel the show and move it to the next day if the storms got bad enough. My mom and I kept our fingers crossed that it wouldn't get any worse. Although it was a bit drizzly and muddy by the time we reached our destination, the weather wasn't too bad.

It was at that particular show I received my "new" name. Someone asked Corey who I was and she responded, "Oh that's Alyx, she's number one in the nation for the Marshall and Sterling Medal." It was a nomenclature that would be used to identify me time and time again in the coming months. I had to admit, I really liked the attention my new name afforded me!

My classes weren't scheduled to start until late in the afternoon so we hoped everything would dry out a bit by the time I was ready to go. I was entered in the two Open Equitation Over Fence classes, which I would use as warm-ups, and the medal. Although the footing in the warm-up area wasn't bad, it didn't take long to see the show ring was quite a different story. As we entered the ring and made our way to the first jump, Jay slipped in the mud. Luckily, I was able to hold him together, but there were several other spots in the course where the same thing happened. On a positive note, one of the outside lines could be ridden as either a forward five or a slow six. When I realized the six wouldn't work, I asked him for the long distance and he didn't hesitate.

As we came out of the ring, my mom could tell we were both shaken by the slippery footing. She advised me to just take my time and not rush anything; under the circumstances my main goal was to be safe. Our second round was much smoother, although after the second jump of the outside line Jay slipped again and I lost my outside rein. I was able to quickly recover it and hid the mistake pretty well. I hoped our medal round would go better.

I was admittedly a bit nervous when they were ready to start the medal class. There were two rollbacks on the course; a tight one at the end of the ring and a broader one across center. Five riders were entered in the class. One of the first riders was disqualified after she fell off. Corey's round was very good, except she got a bad distance on the jump after the first rollback. Another rider had a pretty good round, although her position was a bit too forward. Jay's and my ride was almost flawless, the only exception being when he almost fell to his knees as he slipped in the mud a few strides before the first jump. I just acted as if nothing happened and we continued on. Afterward, the show manager and some others at the in-gate complemented me on my round.

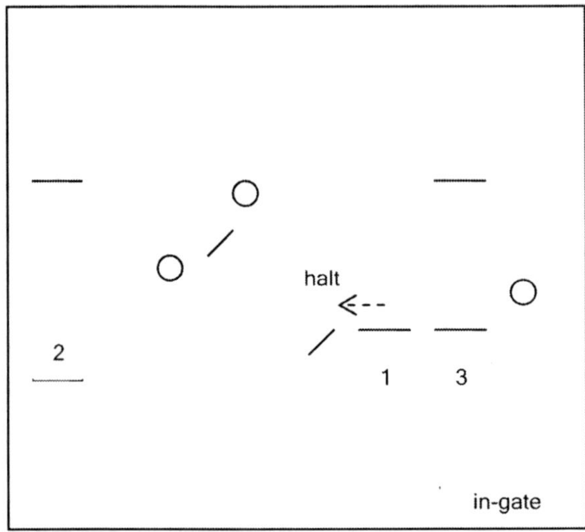

Marshall and Sterling Children's Horse Medal Test

The judge decided on an over fence test for the remaining four riders. We were to canter to jump one, halt, trot the rollback to fence two, canter fence three, then sit trot to the gate. When we were called back I was in first and Corey in third. The first rider did a courtesy circle before starting her course, so my mom and I immediately made sure Corey knew to ignore what she did and go directly to the first jump. In order to make the turn to trot the second jump, the same rider had to halt her horse on the bend. The rest of her ride was pretty good. Corey's test was lovely and we noticed that she had to halt on the bend as well. The second place rider was the only one to stop in a straight line after the first jump, but her position was very forward and her legs weren't strong.

As my turn approached, my mom told me not to try anything fancy in the mud. I needed to take my time and do what was best for my horse. I also ended up halting on the bend, but our transitions were effortless and our ride smooth. There was little doubt in my mind that we'd won the class. When the results were announced, I was first and Corey was second. With the 10 points I'd just earned added to the 94 I already had, I surpassed my 100 point goal for the first half of the year!

I was able to show in a couple of other medal classes in March, but it was April that ended up being a very busy month for Jay and me as we showed in a total of six medal classes. After competing at the Barrington Hill show the last weekend of the month, my point total had risen to 167, even though only 114 of them had been posted as of the April 25th update. The second and third place riders showed 98.5 and 94 points respectively.

Some of the parent's of other riders I normally competed with had voiced concerns to my mom regarding how long it was taking certain shows to send in their points. My mom's response was always the same "don't stress out about it." She encouraged the other parents to keep track of their kids' points and verify them when they were eventually posted to make sure they were correct. She assured them that I had always been accurately credited for all the points I'd accrued, even when those points were sent in late. If results from several months back hadn't been posted by July, then it would be a good idea to touch base with the appropriate show management to follow up. Otherwise, it was best to let things play out as they would.

CHAPTER 20

My Heartbreaking Loss

After a very successful month of April, with all but one first or second place finish in the medal classes, I set a new goal for myself; break 200 points by the end of June. It was an aspiration that seemed well within my reach as my mom went over the May show schedule with me. Since I would be busy with finals and end of year activities at school, our plan was to attend no more than one show a week. For three of the four shows we wouldn't need a stall and I would only be showing in two or three classes; therefore, the cost for each of them would be relatively inexpensive. I think it was at that point I truly believed I was going to finish the year in first place. Of course, amid the best laid plans, situations arose that were completely unexpected.

Sunday, May 20th began like any other horse show day. My mom and I had packed the trailer the night before, so all we had to do that morning was feed the horses, eat breakfast, load Jay into the trailer, and go. While I was getting ready, my mom started cooking breakfast and my dad headed to the barn to feed the horses. About a half hour after I heard my dad close the door to go outside, the radio alert on my mom's cell phone went off. I was already on my way out to the kitchen when I heard her calling me. She told me my dad said Bo was down and wouldn't get up. She said she had seen him walking around the arena through the window just minutes beforehand, and asked if I would go outside to see what was going on since she was still in her pajamas.

When I walked out the door, I could see Bo literally sitting in the arena directly in front of me like a dog. My dad told me he had spent the last fifteen minutes trying to encourage Bo to get up by pulling on his halter with the lead rope, but he wouldn't budge. I walked over to Bo and picked up the lead rope; at which point he tucked his front legs underneath himself and laid down. I knew something was seriously wrong. I ran back up to the house to get my mom. As I walked through the door, she was just hanging up the phone. She had watched me go down to the arena and when she saw what was going on, she knew it was bad. She had immediately called our vets' emergency number and left a message.

In a matter of seconds, she had thrown on her clothes and was headed down to the arena, phone in hand. Shortly thereafter, Donna's colleague Lori called back and my mom filled her in on the situation. She told her she would be over as soon as possible to check Bo; advising us to just let him rest quietly until she got there. While we were waiting for her to arrive, my mom determined that about every ten to fifteen minutes Bo would attempt to get up by himself. He was able to get his front end up, but he seemed to have no strength in his back legs. Since we knew he had arthritis in both his back legs, we thought maybe his right rear leg had become stiff because it was the one he was leaning all his weight on.

When Lori arrived my mom updated her on Bo's situation. She also mentioned that she'd noticed he was laying down more than usual the day before, but had been able to get up and move around without any problem. Armed with all the relevant information, Lori examined Bo. She agreed his right rear leg might be stiff and suggested we roll him over to his other side to see if he would be able to support himself better on his left rear leg. Unfortunately, it made absolutely no difference. He could move his back legs, but he wasn't able to get them under his body to leverage himself enough to lift his hind end up; it was as if his back legs were paralyzed, but not paralyzed.

By that time, Bo had been down over an hour. Lori told us we had to find a way to get him up; otherwise, he could suffer nerve damage in his legs. Not wanting to accept the severity of the situation, I looked at my mom and asked, "What if he doesn't get up?"

Her response sent chills across the back of my neck. "Honey, he has to get up. There is no other option."

A few minutes later Bo attempted to get up by himself again, so we all tried to help him; my mom pulled his front end with the lead rope while my dad, Lori and I supported and pushed his back end to try to lift it off the ground. After another valiant but unsuccessful effort to rise, he lay back down and rolled over on his side exhausted.

Seeing Lori's truck in our backyard, Ernie came over to see what was going on and offer his assistance. For the next hour we tried everything we could think of to encourage him to stand; all to no avail. After each failed attempt to get him on his feet we would let him rest awhile and then when he was ready, try to hoist him up again.

During one of Bo's rest breaks, I headed up to the house to get some tissues. My mom said as soon as I walked through the gate he became very agitated, straining to turn his head back to look at the house. She petted his neck, told him it was okay and assured him I would be right back. As soon as she did he relaxed and laid back down on his side.

Eventually, when he stopped making any effort to work with us, my mom turned to Lori and stated, "It seems like he's not even trying anymore."

Her response was, "I think he's already made his decision."

We'd finally reached a point where we could no longer avoid the inevitable and had to come to terms with the situation. Lori explained that even if we could get Bo to stand up, he would most likely go down again. Fortunately we had been home that morning, but if it had happened after we'd left for the horse show, he could have been down for hours before anyone found him. We all agreed that we owed it to Bo to do the right thing and let him go.

While Lori went to her truck to prepare the injection, my dad brought Cheyenne over so he could say good-bye to his old friend. He immediately put his head down to Bo and sniffed him. Bo responded by turning his head up toward Cheyenne to acknowledge him before laying it back down on the ground. For several more minutes Cheyenne stood quietly next to him. When Lori was ready, my dad brought him back to his stall.

I sat on the ground next to Bo's head and listened while Lori explained everything she was going to do and what I should expect. I really appreciated the fact that she took the time to prepare me the way she did. Before she even started the procedure, Bo had already closed his eyes; he was ready. As Lori administered the injection, I told Bo I loved him and stroked his face while tears streamed down mine. I was surprised at how quickly the drug took effect, his body relaxing as his breathing slowed and eventually stopped.

I had to give my mom credit for keeping herself together throughout the entire episode, especially since I knew it was mostly for my benefit. When it was over Lori hugged her and started crying; that's when she lost it. My dad, and even Ernie, weren't much better off. Once everyone was able to compose themselves, we had to decide what to do next. We were grateful Lori provided us with the phone number of an old family friend who would come out and bury Bo for us. Unable to make the call herself, my mom asked Ernie if he would make the arrangements for us. After doing so, he walked back up to his house to get some old sheets so we could respectfully cover Bo until the man came.

Since there was no way we would be attending the horse show that day, my mom called Jyan and asked her to please let the show office know we wouldn't be able to attend due to our loss. Everyone was so understanding and supportive; we received condolences from Jyan and Corey, Michael and his family, Vicky, Kristine, and the show management at Sumter Equestrian. Of course, the death of a family pet is never easy, but it was nice to know so many people cared.

Bo had always been one of Lori and Donna's favorites; Lori even had one of his Coggins photos set up on her computer's screen saver at home. Knowing that, I was deeply touched when a package arrived in the mail several weeks later containing a beautiful plaque with Bo's picture; a lovely tribute that I placed atop the vanity in my bedroom. When my mom ran into Donna a few weeks later, she admitted she was glad Lori had been on call that day and not her. Understandably, as a vet, she has to euthanize horses due to illness or injury, but she admitted it would have been very difficult for her to do Bo because he was one of the special ones.

I will never forget my beloved Bo and will always cherish my memories of the fun times we spent together. Whether we were out in the woods on one of our adventurous trail rides or participating in the Silver Spurs Rodeo Parade or just hanging out in the backyard; I knew Bo would always watch over and protect me. I like to believe he's still looking out for me from his final resting place on the hillside overlooking our arena and barn. I sometimes think that if he hadn't come into my life, I would never have regained my desire to ride again. For so many years he was my devoted friend and companion; he will always hold a very special place in my heart.

CHAPTER 21

Personal Validation

On the morning of June 17th my mom, dad and I headed to Bushnell for a show at Sumter Equestrian. With the points I'd accumulated since April, I had a grand total of 191 and could conceivably break the 200 mark that day. When we arrived at the showgrounds, the management told my mom that there were only two of us entered in the medal, but since they knew I came specifically for that class they would try to find someone to fill it for me. Just before the class was scheduled to begin, they were able to find a third rider.

Jay and I had a great round and I felt very confident waiting for the test. The judge decided to call all of us in for a work-off on the flat. After several minutes of no stirrup work, she asked one of the riders to move to the middle of the ring while the other rider and I remained on the rail. She continued to put us through our paces for quite some time before asking us to line up in the center of the ring. Due to the oppressive heat and humidity, I had begun to get a little light headed and shaky toward the end of the class. I was so relieved when it was finally over; I just kept saying "thank you, thank you" silently in my mind.

When they announced the placings in reverse order, I was overjoyed to hear I was first. As Jay and I walked out of the ring, my mom congratulated me on breaking 200 points. When the gate person heard her, she teasingly touched my leg as I walked by, made a sizzling sound and said, "Look at you Miss Thing!" We all laughed and I thanked her when she congratulated me.

Once outside the ring I let Jay get a drink of water as I knew he was also feeling the effects of the heat. While waiting for him to finish, we overheard the judge talking to one of the show staff about the class. She said based on the flat test the girl who placed second was a bit ahead of me. What had really been the deciding factor in placing me first was that my over fence portion was so much better than either of the other riders. I was very pleased that Jay and I had done so well over fences because I knew that my flat test was definitely not as good as it could have been.

So much for not wanting to do much showing in the heat of the Florida summer; at least I didn't pass out or get sick on my horse!

On the ride home my mom and I discussed what my plan would be now that I'd reached my second goal for the year. Since the riders up North had so many opportunities to show over the summer, she suggested that I continue to attend as many shows as possible during the next few months to increase my point total. When I asked her if she thought I could reach 300 by the end of the season, she said she didn't know, but it might be fun to see how close I could get. Consequently, getting as close to 300 points as possible by the end of the show year became my next goal.

It was at one of the shows around that time that an individual made the comment to me, "The only reason you're in first place is because you go to a lot of shows."

I tried to explain to them that it didn't necessarily matter how many shows someone went to, they still had to place well to get enough points to keep them at the top of the standings.

Their response was, "That's fine, but I'm going for quality not quantity."

I in turn replied, "Well I'm going for both."

When I later shared what was said with my mom, she was able to immediately put it into perspective for me. She told me to think of it in terms of two riders who each showed in ten medal classes. The first rider placed first in five classes (10 points each) and second in five classes (6 points each). Upon the completion of the ten classes they had a total of 80 points. The second rider placed third in five classes (4 points each) and fourth in five classes (2 points each). They ended up with a total of 30 points. Therefore, consistently placing at the top of each class was crucial to doing well in the standings; the number of classes, although certainly important, was secondary. I felt so much better after we talked and knew I would be more ably prepared to address any similar comments that might be made in the future; although I sincerely hoped it wouldn't come up again.

On June 26th I had to opportunity to attend a riding clinic with Scott Hofstetter at Fox Lea Farm. I had heard so much about his showing and judging experience, as well as his success in training equitation riders, I was really looking forward to having the chance to work with him.

When we arrived at the office to check-in I was extremely happy to find out that they would be holding the clinic in the covered arena due to the heat. After unloading Jay and tacking him up we headed to the ring, arriving just as the first session concluded. A break was scheduled between sessions, so Jay and I found a shady spot under a tree where we could hang out with my mom to wait.

As we waited I became a little anxious, concerned that if I did something wrong Scott might yell at me. Not surprisingly, it had become a bit of a phobia of mine that reared its ugly head whenever I worked with someone new as a result of my experience with Marilyn. Because I'd never met him before, it made the situation even worse. Sensing my uneasiness, my mom told me she was confident I would enjoy the clinic and the opportunity to work with Scott. If by some outside chance he began yelling at me or made me feel uncomfortable, all I had to do was excuse myself and walk out of the arena.

Of course, all of my concerns were completely unfounded. During our first few warm-up exercises I was extremely nervous and stiff; which made Jay behave in a similar fashion. Apparently realizing I was a bit tense as I passed, Scott told me to loosen up my reins all the way to the buckle and just let Jay move around the ring at a nice pace. His calm voice and quiet direction were exactly what I needed to hear; in no time I was completely relaxed and Jay was moving beautifully.

Throughout our session Scott repeatedly told me "very good" or "excellent" as I completed the exercises he gave us. A couple of times he asked me to demonstrate an exercise for him and my efforts were rewarded with comments such as, "that was exactly the way it should be done." I had to admit his remarks were a huge confidence booster.

One thing that truly astounded me during our session was his amazing insight into horses; particularly Thoroughbreds, which I found out later, were his favorite breed. In no time, I could sense that he really "got" Jay and was able to figure out the causes of some of his behaviors. I was amazed that every suggestion he offered immediately impacted Jay's performance in a positive manner; it almost seemed too easy.

Upon the conclusion of our session, several riders including myself spent some time talking to Scott and asking questions. I was quite impressed with how knowledgeable he was and appreciated the fact that he took the time to share his insights into the world of showing with us. Personally I was very grateful for his willingness to answer my multitude of questions regarding what judges look for in equitation and offer suggestions on how to get noticed at the Finals. It was truly an extremely informative and positive experience for me.

On the way home, I mentioned to my mom that I would love to have the opportunity to train with Scott on a regular basis. His depth of knowledge and expertise as a rider, trainer and judge would be invaluable in helping me enhance my skills and achieve my riding goals. She agreed and said that maybe someday I'd have the chance to work with him again. I certainly hoped so.

A couple of weeks after the clinic, one of my greatest fears became a reality at the July FHCA show. As usual, since it was being held at Canterbury it was a two-day show on Saturday and Sunday with the medal class offered both days. Much to everyone's consternation, the weather on Saturday turned out to be absolutely hideous. Several times throughout the day, management had to stop the show and hold all classes due to the severe thunderstorms that were moving through the area. And the storms didn't move quickly through; each weather-related incident held everything up for at least an hour.

By the time they were ready to start the 2'9" and 3' divisions, it was already nearly 8:30 pm with another incoming storm approaching from the west. Rather than keep the show going late into the night, management decided to re-schedule the remainder of Saturday's classes for first thing Sunday morning before the start of the regular schedule. Some riders and trainers were extremely upset by the decision, but I personally had no desire to brave the elements and was more than happy to wait until morning.

The next day dawned bright and sunny, although the humidity was miserable even at 7:00 am. Since it had rained heavily on and off throughout the evening, the main warm-up ring was completely underwater by morning. As a result, several practice jumps had been set up in the grassy area next to the covered arena for us to school over.

Due to the modifications to the schedule, I would only be showing in three classes; a 3' hunter class which would be our warm-up, followed by the two medal classes. Jay and I schooled over the jumps in the grass before our first class and we ended up having a very good hunter round that earned us second place in a class of six. There was some confusion with the schedule shortly thereafter, which ended up causing a significant amount of time to pass between my hunter class and the first medal class. Given that Jay had been standing around for quite a while, my mom told me to work him a little on the flat and take him over a couple of jumps to wake him up.

I walked Jay over to the grassy area and proceeded to trot him around a bit. Just as we picked up the canter and were making the turn away from the arena, Jay slipped in some thick brown, slimy muck that had accumulated in a low area. It immediately became one of those moments that seemed to move in slow motion. He lost his footing on his front end, went down on his right knee and then his left, right before his nose hit the ground. As he was going down, I braced myself in my stirrups and pulled back as hard as I could in an attempt to get his head up; afraid he was going to flip over. In the distance I could hear a collective gasp from the crowd of people behind me next to the ring. Jay somehow managed to quickly get his front feet back under his body, but after he did so, he leaped straight up into the air and let go with a huge buck as he came down. Thrown off balance, I lost a stirrup and started slipping sideways. All I could do was grab at his mane, my saddle and anything else I could get my hands on in order to avoid falling off. I don't know how I did it, but I was able to pull myself back into the saddle and bring him to a halt as he tried to run off. As we both stood there shaking, one of the trainers yelled over, "Way to hang on!" I just looked at her with what must have been deer in the headlight eyes and nodded in acknowledgement.

It was probably a good thing that my mom had been looking in the opposite direction as we went down. When she heard the gasp from the crowd, she turned just in time to see Jay launch into air before he landed and bucked. As she made her way over to me her face was drained of all color, just as I imagined mine was. After I explained what happened, she said I was done schooling in the grass. Following her, we walked over to the side of the ring so she could check Jay's legs and shoes to make sure he was okay.

Physically we may have come out of our falling episode unscathed, but mentally was a different story and I was extremely nervous about going into the ring. Before I knew it though, I was told it was my turn to go in for the first medal class. Jay was still a bit shaken from the fall too, but at least he seemed willing to work with me. Our round was actually going quite well until we came around the turn by the in-gate off the outside line as we made our way to the opposite inside line. I asked him for a lead change as we passed the in-gate, but he didn't swap his back end. When I tried to skip him into it as we turned to approach the inside line, he broke stride and trotted two steps. With twelve riders in the class, I knew we had just lost any chance of pinning. I was very disappointed when we left the ring, but at least we had gotten through the course. All things considered, Jay handled it much better than I thought he would.

Our second medal class was quite the opposite. By the time we entered the ring any anxiety Jay and I had been experiencing was gone. To help save time and keep the show moving, a test had already been built into the course. Halfway through we had to canter an inside single, halt, back, reverse, and trot back over the single. Jay performed everything quietly and calmly, and our turn on the haunches to reverse was flawless. I was so proud of him! We ended up pinning second out of twelve and I couldn't have been happier after what we had been through earlier.

CHAPTER 22

The Long Road to Georgia

As we neared the end of the Marshall and Sterling show season, my mom decided it would be a good idea to make a long distance trip as sort of a "test run" to see how both she and Jay would handle being on the road for an extended period of time. In checking the show calendar, she discovered that a Georgia Hunter Jumper Association show offering the medal class was scheduled the weekend of my sixteenth birthday, August 11th. We were both excited to find out it was being held at the Georgia International Horse Park in Conyers, the former Olympic site, since neither one of us had ever been there before. In addition to testing our endurance on the road, we both felt the trip would be a good indicator of how Jay would handle showing in an unfamiliar place, particularly because it was something he hadn't done in quite some time.

On Friday, August 10th my mom, Jay, Merrill, Suzu, and I headed north on our very first out of state horse show. We checked and double checked the car and trailer several times before we left to ensure we had all of the necessary horse show accoutrements, including the appropriate paperwork. After nearly eight grueling hours on the road with a couple of stops for breaks and gas, we finally reached our destination.

As we drove through the Horse Park, my mom and I commented how nicely it was laid out and how beautifully the grounds were kept. I loved the oval shaped barns and as I caught glimpses of the rings, my anticipation began to build. I was really looking forward to having a chance to show there; that was until, I opened the car door to take the dogs out for a walk while my mom checked-in at the office. The intense heat was indescribable and after hours of sitting in the air conditioned car, the shock of it jolted my entire body. We found out shortly thereafter that although it was nearly 5:00 pm, the temperature outside was approximately 103 degrees with a heat index of 110 degrees. I couldn't believe it; it was hotter in Georgia than it had been in Florida! The dogs and I wasted little time taking care of their doggie needs before quickly scrambling back inside truck to take advantage its cool interior.

After checking in, the show manager took my mom on a tour of the grounds in her golf cart. When Vickie found out we had driven all the way up from Central Florida in preparation for our trip to New York and that I was the number one ranked rider, she was genuinely very excited for me. Once my mom returned we quickly unloaded the trailer, set up Jay's stall, and tacked him up for a quick schooling session. As Jay and I waited for our turn outside one of the rings, Vickie made a point to introduce me to some of the other riders, their families and trainers. I have to say I was a little embarrassed at being treated like a celebrity, but Vickie and everyone else at the show were all so friendly and helpful I felt as if I had known them for years.

Because we'd been on the road for so long, we kept schooling to a minimum. My goal was just to familiarize Jay with the surroundings, the ring and the jumps. I have to say, the jumps they had set up in the show rings were some of the most beautiful I had ever seen. There were jumps with elegant columns, intricately detailed walls, standards shaped like barns, huge hanging planters, and other lovely decorations. And the best thing about them was Jay didn't even give them a second glance. I was very encouraged by the way he handled himself and was starting to think New York was not going to be a problem.

To make Jay more comfortable we set up two fans on his stall to ensure we kept the air circulating in the stifling heat. Later that evening as we watched the news in our trailer, the weather reporter said Saturday would be even hotter with temperatures around 105 degrees and a heat index of 115 degrees. My mom told me that depending on how hot it was and how quickly the show was moving, she might scratch a couple of classes I was scheduled to show in. With the temperatures so high there was no reason to risk either Jay or me being overcome by the heat.

We headed over to the barn around 8:00 am the following morning and it was already horrendous outside! Although the humidity level was definitely lower than back home, the extreme temperatures seemed to suck the energy right out of you. Since she didn't want either Jay or me to overdo it, my mom immediately made the decision we would just show in a flat equitation class and the medal. She also suggested I head down to the dark, cool recesses of the covered arena to warm-up for our classes instead of the open area next to the show ring.

When I finally entered the ring for my first class, I was thrilled that Jay was calm and quiet. I was quite relieved it was a flat class because I was really feeling the effects of the heat for some reason and could tell my position wasn't as solid as it usually was. I still finished fourth out of eight though, so it wasn't too bad.

Since it would be quite some time before the medal class commenced, my mom began pumping me with Gatorade and fruit. As we got closer to the start of my class, I was feeling much better and definitely wasn't as shaky as I had been earlier. Thus fortified, I headed to the covered arena to warm-up over fences. Jay schooled beautifully and I was confident we would do well.

Once in the ring, my medal class was going great until we were about midway through the course. We had just come off a jump on the outside line and were heading around the end of the ring to approach an inside line. To provide some respite from the sun and heat, quite a few spectators had set up canopies along the ring's perimeter. Just as we were passing one of them on our left side, several people lifted it up off the ground in order to disassemble it. Jay immediately spooked and jumped to his right. Luckily I was able to keep him moving forward, but in the process he swapped his lead. I quickly asked him to swap it back to the correct one as we made our turn to the next line, which he did. He was still a little tense from the episode and several strides out from the jump he swapped back to the incorrect lead and bumped the rail as he went over. It was unfortunate, but I was very thankful we placed second, even with the mistakes.

The next day was decidedly cooler; much to everyone's relief. The only problem was we had to deal with some very unseasonable and blustery winds. Again, Jay and I were having a wonderful medal round and were down to the last two jumps. The obstacles were positioned on opposite ends of the ring and after jumping the first one you had to ride diagonally across the ring, go halfway around the far end, then turn to a jump positioned toward the center of the ring. Seeing as there was so much distance to cover between the two, my plan had been to hand gallop to the last jump.

We got over the first fence perfectly and I had just asked Jay to open his stride for the hand gallop. As we passed a jump on our left with large planters hanging from the standards, a strong gust of wind blew one of the baskets sideways at us causing the long leafy tendrils of the plant to blow out toward us just inches from my leg. It couldn't have been worse timing! Jay must have caught sight of it out of the corner of his eye and thought a flying green monster with tentacles was attacking him. He sidestepped away from the offending foliage and then shifted into hyper-drive, galloping across the ring and around the corner at breakneck speed. I literally had to fight with him as I attempted to slow him down and regain control. Finally, just as we made the turn toward the last jump, I was able to calm him down and re-engage his brain. By that point though I didn't have enough time or room to gather him up and collect him. Not surprisingly, he was rather hesitant going into the jump and a bit flat as he left the ground which caused him to pull the rail. At least there were only three riders in the class that day and third out of three was better than nothing.

As my mom and I talked about the show on our way back to Florida, we were actually both quite pleased with the way everything turned out. Although Jay had a couple of extremely stressful moments in the medal classes due to the unusual circumstances, he had still been willing to follow my directions and finish the courses. He trusted me to get us through them even though he had his doubts. I knew very well that weird things you weren't prepared for could happen any time you were in the ring and you just had to keep going as if nothing had happened. After our experience that weekend, I knew without a doubt that Jay and I would be able to conquer anything we faced up in New York.

CHAPTER 23

National Finals - Here We Come

I attended a couple more shows in the following weeks, and when the show season finally ended on September 2nd I had accumulated a total of 293 points! Based on my show record, I finished either first or second in 70% of all the medal classes I'd competed in during the year. By the September 5th update to the standings, 283 of my points had been posted. My mom had been tracking the standings as they were updated each week throughout the year and since climbing to the top of the rankings on January 26th, I had never relinquished my first place position.

After so many months of practicing and hard work, the realization that I'd achieved my primary goal was beginning to sink in. Not only had I finished the year ranked as the number one rider in the country, I had earned nearly double the points of the previous year's champion and had accrued over 100 points more than the closest rider in the standings. In our pursuit of points, Jay and I had competed in eight different circuits/series, as well as, some individual shows across the state of Florida and beyond. I was quite proud of the fact that we had been consistently successful no matter where we showed. My achievement was incontestable; we had triumphed based on our merit and skill.

Over time I had come to sincerely appreciate the independence and flexibility I was afforded by not having to rely on a having a trainer present when I competed. My mom and I could come and go as we pleased and attend whatever shows worked for us. Having the ability to compete in a wide variety of shows at different venues had been instrumental in helping me not only accrue points, but gain valuable experience in the ring for myself and Jay.

As we began our preparations for the journey north to the Finals, my mom began to experience some feelings of insecurity about our upcoming endeavor. She was very concerned about driving to New York and back without another licensed driver traveling with us. She was afraid that if something happened to her, I would be left alone to deal with the situation. Driving up didn't bother her as much as the trip back because she believed the adrenaline rush from the anticipation of showing in a national final would keep her going. After a week at the showgrounds, when all the excitement over, she feared she might be too tired to drive all the way back to Florida by herself.

She also started to worry she might do something that would negatively affect me if she acted as my trainer at the show. For some reason she felt there would be certain special protocols that had to be followed at the Finals and she could potentially commit a serious faux pas that would be detrimental to me as a rider. I tried to tell her time and time again that we would be okay, but as our departure date got closer she just kept getting more stressed out. I assured her we didn't need anyone else; it was just another horse show and we would be fine by ourselves. I reminded her that for nearly four years, with only a few exceptions, she had been my trainer at every show. She had done just as good a job as any other trainer, if not better. There was no need to worry; I had utmost confidence in her and her ability to coach me.

Sadly, she didn't have confidence in herself. Several days before we were supposed to leave, she made arrangements to fly Kristine up to Albany the day before the awards party. Kristine agreed to stay in the trailer with us to help keep expenses down and would accompany us on the drive home. While at the show she would coach me during my Hudson Equitation and Medal Final classes.

Thinking that my mom would be feeling better about the entire trip, I was rather surprised to find out she had arranged for Corey's trainer, Denna, to school me during my ticketed warm-ups. Because Kristine's lesson schedule didn't allow her to fly up before Thursday, my mom felt she needed someone else to work with me when I went into the Grand Prix ring to practice. Again, I told her I would be fine with her coaching me, but she was insistent.

I really felt bad about her lack of self-confidence because I never would have been able to accomplish everything I had without her at my side every single step of the way. Each time Jay and I had come up against some obstacle in our training, she found ways to help us get past them so we could move forward. When others tried to shake my confidence in myself or my horse, she was there to rebuild and strengthen it. Her resolve to do whatever she could to make my dream a reality was unwavering. I knew no matter what happened she would always be there for me; that was all I really needed.

CHAPTER 24

2007 Marshall and Sterling Finals

September 9 – 11, 2007

Sunday morning, September 9th dawned bright and sunny. After some last minute packing, my mom, Jay, Merrill, Suzu, and I bid my dad adieu and began our extended journey to Saugerties, New York and the Marshall and Sterling Finals. After ten hours in on the road we arrived at our first overnight stop in Hope Mills, North Carolina at the Horsetel. We'd hoped it would be little cooler there than it had been back home, but it was actually hotter!

The owner of the farm, Patty, had everything ready for our arrival and proved to be a very gracious and accommodating hostess. Since Jay had been cooped up in the trailer for so long, she let us turn him out in a paddock for a couple of hours so he could stretch his legs before we fed him and tucked him in for the night. She had water and electric available for us to hook-up our trailer right next to the barn, which proved to be extremely convenient. During the night she checked on Jay for us to make sure he was okay, and in the morning left us a night watch report and some treats for him.

We left North Carolina early Monday morning and arrived at Farrington Farms in North Brunswick, New Jersey after a nine and a half hour trip. Gary, the owner, was out front to meet us when we arrived and he had a stall already set up for Jay with hay and water. After chatting with him and his wife Sue for a while, we found out that their son Brian would also be competing at the Finals in the Children's Hunter division. Once Jay was settled in his accommodations, my mom, the dogs and I headed for a local hotel. We were both looking forward to having a chance to sleep in a little later the following morning as the showgrounds were only about two and a half hours away.

I had spoken to Jyan Monday afternoon, and she, Corey and Peter were already at the showgrounds awaiting the arrival of Mickey the next day. They had decided to send her up using a commercial shipper rather than haul her up themselves. Jyan assured us we'd have cooler weather up at the showgrounds; something I was looking forward to since it was in the upper 80's and humid even in New Jersey. After talking to her, I felt a twinge of sadness. I really wished my dad had been able to join us on the trip, but knew it hadn't been possible.

We were glad we got a pretty early start Tuesday morning because we had to deal with incessant rain all the way to Saugerties. When we arrived at the HITS on the Hudson showgrounds we almost had to swim to the barn; the grounds were a giant mud pit. Surprisingly, not many people had arrived yet, so the majority of the stalls were empty. We quickly unloaded Jay and all of the necessary equipment, hay and feed. By the time we had finished, my mom and I were completely drenched.

As if perfectly timed, Corey and Jyan met up with us right after my mom returned from checking in at the office. After sharing some interesting stories about the trip from Florida to New York, they directed us to the RV area so we could park our trailer next to the motorhome they'd rented. Once everything was set up, my mom climbed into bed for a much needed nap while Corey and I explored the showgrounds.

At an FHCA show back in August, we found out that another rider we were friendly with from that circuit, Sarah, had also qualified for the Medal Finals and would be joining us at the show. Although she hadn't arrived yet, we assumed the empty stall across from Jay's was for her horse, Jocko. As I walked through the barn with Corey, I was happy to find out that other Florida riders we knew were assigned stalls around us; including a couple Denna's pony riders, Michael, one of his mom's students, and some riders from the Tampa area. It would definitely be nice to see so many familiar faces up there.

While my mom and I had been setting up the trailer, Mickey had arrived. Corey and I spent some time talking to people in the barn and once it stopped raining about mid-afternoon we took Jay and Mickey out to the paddocks. After they had a chance to expend some of their pent up energy, we went for a little trail ride around the showgrounds to acclimate them to their surroundings. On the way back, Mickey decided she wasn't at all thrilled with her environs and couldn't wait to get back to the barn. While Corey brought her back, I decided to head over to the Grand Prix ring to take a look at it from ground level. Gazing out across its vast expanse from the in-gate, it didn't seem quite as big as it did the previous year for some reason. I had a feeling though that I'd probably take those words back once I had a chance to school in there the next morning with Jay.

September 12, 2007

Listening to the morning news, my mom and I were happy to hear the forecast called for sunshine and temperatures in the mid-70's, especially after all the rain and dreariness of the day before. It was at that time we also heard that they were expecting temperatures to drop down into the 40's Friday morning; way too cold for a girl born and raised in Florida! I knew from past experience that I didn't handle the cold well and it had a definite impact on my performance when I was showing. Maybe it would be one of those times when the meteorologists were way off on their forecast; I could only hope.

After feeding Jay and tacking him up, my mom and I headed over to the schooling area by the Grand Prix ring to meet Denna for my warm-up. I again tried to tell my mom that she was perfectly capable of helping me practice, but she said she'd already made the arrangements and it wouldn't be fair to cancel at the last minute.

Corey was already in the schooling area, and having finished her flatwork, was ready to begin jumping. When she noticed I had arrived, Denna asked me to start warming up on the flat. My mom climbed the stairs to make her way to the top of the berm where she stood with Jyan and watched us practice.

Jay acted as though he been there a hundred times before; nothing really seemed to faze him in the schooling area. I worked him at the walk, trot and canter until Denna was ready for me to practice over fences. While I took a few jumps under her watchful eye, Corey and Mickey walked around the perimeter of the schooling area. When we were sufficiently warmed-up, we headed to the Grand Prix ring. I have to admit I was very thankful that we had a chance to warm-up in the schooling area before even attempting the show ring as it really helped me relax. Of course, my anxiety rose a bit as we headed toward the in-gate.

Corey went in first and I had to laugh at the look of utter shock on Mickey's face as she walked under the bridge and into the arena. Once inside though, she was all business. I prayed that Jay would follow her lead and proceed without incident. Of course, that was not the case. Just as he was about to walk under the bridge, Jay decided it wasn't in his best interest and stopped dead in his tracks. I tried to encourage him to move forward, but he refused to budge. Seeing my dilemma, my mom walked down to where we were standing, took Jay's reins, patted him, told him it was okay, and led him into the ring. After we were well past the bridge, my mom released him and went back up to the berm to watch us.

I turned Jay to the right and asked him to walk alongside the stone wall that surrounded the arena. Although he initially seemed a bit concerned about some of the planters situated along the top of the wall, as my anxiety dissipated, so did his. We followed the wall along the ring's perimeter at the trot and then turned around and went in the opposite direction. I cantered around the jumps a bit and then walked Jay over to the gazebo in the center of the ring so he could get a good look at it. When I was ready, I joined Denna for some jumping practice.

I couldn't have been more pleased with the way Jay behaved during our warm-up. Although he pulled one rail when we first started jumping, he happily went over every single fence I put in front of him. He performed everything I asked calmly and efficiently. When we rode lines he nailed the strides every time. There was no spooking, refusing or running out. Afterward, as we headed back to the barn, Denna complimented Jay and me by saying we'd done a great job. Even though I wasn't her student, she didn't treat me any differently than she did Corey. She encouraged me, offered suggestions and made it a completely positive experience; something I sincerely appreciated.

I had to admit though, riding in the Grand Prix ring for the first time was an extremely daunting experience. I'd never shown or ridden in anything that could even compare to it, especially the sheer size. I was convinced it would be an absolutely amazing experience once I was able to actually show in it over the weekend. Back at the barn, my mom showed me some pictures she had taken of Jay and me while we were practicing. We looked so small amid the great expanse of the ring, it was a bit overwhelming.

Corey and I had homework assignments to work on, so we gave the horses the afternoon off and turned them out in the paddocks. I was so glad my mom reserved the paddock for Jay as I knew he'd really appreciate the time out of his stall. He was used to being outside about twelve hours a day at home and with the incredibly beautiful weather we were experiencing, I knew he'd really enjoy hanging out in the paddock watching the comings and goings around the barn.

My mom and I headed back to the barn later that afternoon with the dogs in tow to feed Jay his dinner. I was quite surprised to see that most of the stalls had almost magically filled to capacity virtually in a matter of hours. What a difference from the day before when the barns were still relatively empty and an overall calmness prevailed over the area. Even that morning, the Grand Prix ring had seemed like our own private domain with only a few riders practicing. The atmosphere had definitely changed since then; the showgrounds now hummed with activity as people, horses and trailers converged in a sort of organized chaos. For the first time since we'd arrived, I felt a sense of excitement building within the barn that seemed to be a living, breathing entity unto itself.

When we got to Jay's stall we discovered that Sarah and her family had arrived very late the previous evening. Her mom, Lisa, had just arrived to feed her horse. Jocko's stall was across and down a bit from Jay's and we hadn't even noticed him that morning. We chatted with Lisa for a little while before she was ready to head back to the hotel. Naturally, they were very tired after their long drive and had decided to take it easy that day. We planned to meet back at the barn in the morning so Sarah could school with Corey and me.

Denna arrived at the barn a while later and advised us that schooling for the ticketed warm-ups the next day would be limited to small groups of riders at specific fence heights. Each group would be limited to about eight minutes in the ring so we would really have to use our time wisely. We would only be allowed to go over designated jumps, so even though they had set up more obstacles on both sides of the ring, the ones available for schooling would be limited.

I think it was at that point the realization I would be competing in a national final finally hit me. As my mom and I walked back to the trailer and I looked around at all the accoutrements of the show barns from around the country that decorated the area, a feeling of exhilaration began to build within me. There I was the backyard rider who was not affiliated with any show barn, surrounded by riders who worked with some of the most renowned trainers in the country. I had worked extremely hard during the past year against some pretty tough odds, but I never once faltered in my determination to be number one in the nation. Walking through the area, I felt a deep sense of pride swell within me as I reflected on what Jay and I had accomplished together. As I did so, I became a little teary eyed.

September 13, 2007

We headed over to the barn at 8:00 am since we wanted to get an early start in the Grand Prix ring before it got too busy. Much to my extreme dismay, it was a whopping 48 degrees that morning! I was very thankful that Jyan had volunteered to feed Jay for us bright and early at 5:30 am. We'd heard on the radio they were anticipating temperatures in the 30's Saturday or Sunday morning; I was convinced it was a plot to torture all the Florida riders.

Corey, Sarah and I were in one of the first groups to enter the ring for the warm-up. Jay went in completely relaxed and schooled even better than he had the day before. He was absolutely perfect! I was so pleased with him; there he was a thousand miles away from home, in a place he'd never been before, working in an enormous ring, and he calmly did everything I'd asked without question.

The only thing I was a little apprehensive about was the scoreboard at the back side of the ring up on the berm. Apparently, during the warm-ups the previous afternoon they had turned it on and the clicking noise it made every time the display changed spooked some of the horses. Both times I'd been in the ring it was turned off, so I was concerned that it might be a challenge once we start showing. I just had to hope that Jay would ignore it.

After another very positive and productive schooling session with Denna, Corey, Sarah and I took our horses on a trail ride along a road at the back of the property. The path was essentially a big loop that passed through some lovely countryside. The only problem we ran into was some standing water next to a lake that the horses refused to traverse. Sarah attempted to go through first and Jocko emphatically said, "No way!" Jay's reaction was unquestionably the same. Corey felt it wasn't worth tempting fate, so we decided to turn around and head toward the safety of the showgrounds. We ended up taking a meandering route back to our barn by way of the paddocks and the lower barns, stopping to chat for a while in one of the grassy areas along the way.

Upon our return to the barn, I untacked Jay and turned him out in the paddock. My mom and I then spent the early afternoon at a thoroughly exciting and stimulating place, the local Laundromat. I'd never had the pleasure of visiting one before and it was a whole new experience for me. Amid waves of excruciating boredom, I entertained myself by watching the dials click through the cycles on the washers and the timers go down minute by minute on the dryers. It certainly gave me a whole new appreciation for being able to just drop my clothes in the washer or dryer at home and then go off to do other things. After a couple of hours we finally finished our clothes; just in time to head up to Albany to pick Kristine up from the airport.

Back at the trailer we met up with Corey who joined my mom, Kristine, the dogs, and me for a stroll up to the office to pick up our tickets for the year-end awards party the following evening. On the board outside the office they had posted the order of go for all of the next day's classes and the year-end top ten standings for each Marshall and Sterling division. My mom read the placings for the Children's Horse Medal and a look of panic momentarily appeared on her face. They had posted them in reverse order from tenth to first and she didn't realize it when she initially looked at the list. Once she started breathing again, she was able to see that I would be receiving the Grand Champion honors and Corey the ninth place award. It was finally official!

Later that evening our friends from Chicago, Keith and Debbie, called to let us know their plane had landed in Albany and they had arrived safely. Keith had worked with my mom for over ten years, and he and his wife had flown in to spend the weekend with us and watch me compete for the first time. I hadn't seen either of them in nearly a year and was looking forward to spending time with them.

September 14, 2007

With no more ticketed warm-ups available and my first class scheduled for the next day, my mom and I met Keith and Debbie at their hotel to embark on a sightseeing excursion to Rhinebeck, New York, home of the Old Rhinebeck Aerodrome. My mom and Keith had been talking about visiting the museum for weeks, but I wasn't the least bit convinced it would have a big fun factor for me. Once we started walking through the buildings though, I was rather intrigued. It was fascinating to see all the old antique airplanes and engines and learn how air transportation developed in the early years. I had to give credit to the pioneers of aviation; they were undeniably, extremely brave souls.

After a delicious lunch at an Italian restaurant in the area and a visit to the local bookstore, we left Keith and Debbie at their hotel. They were planning to join us for the awards party and wanted to relax a little before the evening's festivities. We said our goodbyes, made sure they had the directions to the showgrounds, and then headed back to Saugerties.

My mom and I arrived in time to watch some of the hunter classes late that afternoon. I was extremely surprised by the number of horses that refused or ran out on course, resulting in an automatic score of 40. After witnessing quite a few of those mishaps, I made a commitment to myself that when I eventually had the chance to show I was not going to allow Jay to refuse or run out on any jumps; no matter what it took to get him over.

A couple of hours later, after we had all changed and freshened up a bit, the event I had been waiting for all year arrived! Keith and Debbie met us at our trailer, joining my mom, Kristine and I as we walked to the pavilion next to the Grand Prix ring for the year-end awards celebration. As they had the previous year, Tavern on the Green catered the event and we were treated to a wide variety of culinary delights. Corey, Jyan and Peter joined us for dinner as we filled up on the delectable cuisine. We were very happy to find out from them, that in addition to winning 9th place in the Children's Horse Medal division, Corey also picked up the 10th place award in the Children's Hunter Horse division.

My anticipation grew exponentially with each passing minute. By the time Tom Struzzerri took the stage for the year-end award presentations, I could barely sit in my chair. The Children's Horse Medal was the third or fourth division to be presented, and as he had with the previous divisions, Tom called the award recipients to the stage in order from tenth to first place amid rounds of applause. When we had all assembled next to him, he told the audience that the Children's Horse Medal had been the most competitive of all the Marshall and Sterling divisions in

2007. I was so excited when the audience applauded enthusiastically in response to his statement my legs started shaking!

After the tenth through second place riders were presented their awards, I was called up for the Grand Champion honors. A representative from Marshall and Sterling Insurance presented me with a gorgeous ribbon and silver framed award certificate, both of which had also been given to each of the top ten riders. In addition, I received an embroidered jacket and a letter from Essex Classics for a riding shirt. While I was receiving my awards, the area around us exploded with flashing lights as a multitude of people took our picture. It was kind of weird, but very cool! When I got back to my seat, my mom laughingly said we could go home because I got my jacket.

Moments later I was invited over to an area that had been set up with a special backdrop for photos. I stood there for quite some time as people took what seemed like a hundred photos; I had them taken with my mom, Kristine, Corey, and other Florida riders. Every time I thought I was done, I'd be called back for more. Quite frankly, it was rather nice being a celebrity for the evening and the recipient of so much attention. Once the awards presentation concluded, Suzanne Vega performed some of her songs. We ended up staying for most of her performance before we finally gave in and decided to call it a night. Later, as I lay in bed thinking about the evening's events, I knew the memory of it was one I would treasure the rest of my life!

September 15, 2007

My first class, the Hudson Equitation Classic, was scheduled for 4:30 in the afternoon after the completion of some of the other divisions, so we had quite a long wait. Corey had kindly offered to braid Jay for my classes and when I saw him standing in his stall that morning with his formal hairdo, I had to admit he looked quite handsome.

As the time approached for my class, Jay and I joined Kristine in one of the side rings to warm-up. My mom had made a point to specifically review with her how we prepared for our classes. I would always warm Jay up on the flat, take a couple of jumps at 2'6", then some more at 3'. When he'd gone over them consistently well, my mom would raise the jump to either 3'3" or 3'6" as a reminder to him to pick up his feet. She told Kristine he would probably either bump or pull the rail the first or second time, but after that he usually worked it out. Once he took the higher jump nicely a couple of times and we could end on a positive note, he was ready to go into the ring.

So as not to interfere with Kristine's direction, my mom stood on berm to watch me from a distance with Keith and Debbie. Kristine followed my mom's instructions and we had a really good warm-up. Making my way to the in-gate, I signaled for my mom to come down next to me. I told her I wanted her to stay with me at the in-gate and not watch from the side. She agreed without hesitation and handed Keith our camera so he could video tape me from the higher vantage on top of the berm.

It may sound silly, but I had come to always expect that my mom would be standing near the in-gate when I was showing and would get upset if I didn't see her. There had been a couple of times in the past that she had been video taping me in a class and had moved to the side of the ring for a better angle. When I glanced toward the in-gate during my course and didn't see her, I started to panic and lose focus. As I would land after each jump, I would immediately start looking around until I caught sight of her. It was not a situation conducive to my performing effectively on horseback. The last time she had done it was at the beginning of the year when I was showing Riley in a jumper class. I was so stressed out by the time I exited the ring, I literally begged her not to do it again; and up to that point, she hadn't. The Finals were no exception, even if Kristine was there; I wanted my mom with me at the in-gate.

To get all sixty some odd riders through the class relatively quickly, they split the riders into A and B groups, and then set up dividers across the middle of the arena to create two separate courses. Corey and I were in group A on the left side of the arena and Sarah was in group B on the right side. I was able to watch Corey go, but didn't get a chance to see Sarah; although she did tell me later Jocko had a hard time standing still in the in-gate and pulled a rail on course.

When it was finally my turn to go, I was so nervous I wanted to cry. Jay did a great job getting perfect distances, making all the strides and clearing each jump with room to spare; although he did get a little looky at a five foot high green and white box with pumpkins and flowers surrounding its base. I, on the other hand, was stiff in my upper body throughout the entire course. I was happy though because we got through it without any problems. Again, I was stunned by the number of horses that refused and ran out; even ones that were in the top of the standings. All things considered, even though we didn't pin, we held our own and I was very happy.

September 16, 2007

We were welcomed with 38 degree temperatures the morning of the Final. It was extremely cold by Florida standards and very windy. All I could do was layer my clothes in an attempt to stay warm. The Children's Horse Medal was scheduled to follow the Pony Medal at 11:30 am and I was 12th in the order of go.

In addition to our friends Keith and Debbie, my uncle, aunt, cousins and family friends were planning to drive over from Connecticut to watch me compete. I was really looking forward to seeing my mom's brother Skip and his wife Cathy as it had been quite a few years since they'd been down to Florida for a visit. Even though they'd seen me ride before, they'd never met Jay nor had they seen me compete. As if pre-planned, everyone arrived at the showgrounds within minutes of each other. Since it was only about 9:00 am I was able bring them all to the barn to introduce them to Jay.

Keith and Debbie arrived as our group was walking back to the vendor area. While my cousins and their friends looked around the shops, the rest of us stopped at the café for some food and hot drinks. Afterward, we scoped out a spot on the side of the berm where the judge's booth was located, appropriated enough chairs for our entire group and watched the final riders in the Pony Medal compete. I really enjoyed having time to relax and visit with everyone before I had to get ready.

When the Pony Medal concluded, the jump crew entered the ring to make some changes and raise the jumps. The Children's Medal riders were then given the opportunity to walk the course, so Kristine and I headed down to the ring to develop our strategy. The course consisted of fifteen jumps, including a bending line of four jumps and two in-and-outs. Knowing Jay did well in tight turns, we decided I would take the inside line on several of the rollbacks. I was feeling decidedly more confident than I had the previous day. My goal had been to compete in the national finals and there I was walking the course with Kristine. Obviously I wanted to do well, but more importantly, I wanted to get through the course with no refusals or run outs. Once we finished strategizing, Kristine, my mom and I hurried back to the barn to get Jay ready.

By the time we returned to the schooling area to warm-up, I was already eight riders out; they were moving a lot faster than we had anticipated. I immediately started working Jay on the flat and could feel my stress level build as we rushed through our exercises. He schooled very well and didn't seem to be bothered by the chaos around him or my anxiety. In minutes we were ready to take a jump Kristine had set up for us at 3'. While Jay and I practiced, my mom waited by the in-gate to monitor how quickly they were moving.

After taking several good jumps, Kristine raised the rail to 3'3" for us so we could finish our warm-up. As I took Jay around the ring for another approach, my mom walked over to let her know I was four riders out. Standing on the side of the standard, they watched as Jay and I cleared the fence two times without even rubbing it. Riding around the corner of the ring, I heard Kristine call out to me to come around and take it one more time. Unknowingly to me, she proceeded to raise the jump even higher. Not anticipating an alteration to our normal schooling routine, neither Jay nor I expected the change in fence height. I didn't even realize it had been raised until we were a stride or two out; by then it was too late. Jay lifted off the ground and hit the jump pole so hard with both front legs as he went over, he sent it flying out in front of us. It bounced and rolled underneath him as we landed, before eventually came to rest about fifteen feet in front of the jump. Jay scrambled over it and proceeded to take off galloping through the crowd of horses and riders in front of us. I was relieved I was able to stop him at the end of the ring without incident. We were both extremely upset by what had occurred, so I hurried back toward Kristine, anxious to let her know we needed to take the jump again.

My mom told me later that she had immediately asked Kristine if the jump was 3'6" because it looked really high. Her response had been that it was at least 3'9". Completely stressing out, my mom explained to her that Jay had to take it again before going in the ring. I quickly made my way to over to them and reiterated the same thing; we had to take the jump again. Kristine disagreed with us and said she wanted his legs to sting when he went into the ring so he'd remember to pick his feet up. My mom tried to make her understand that we always made sure Jay took at least one good jump before going into the ring; we never sent him into the ring on a pulled rail. Mentally, both Jay and I had to conclude our warm-up on a positive note. In the midst of their heated discussion we heard the gate person announce that I was one out and needed to get to the in-gate immediately, effectively putting an end to the debate. I had no alternative but to head over to the ring and wait for my turn.

CHAPTER 25

2007 Marshall and Sterling Children's Horse Medal Final

As soon as Jay and I enter the ring, I can sense he's extremely agitated. Sitting atop him, I can feel the tension in his body and he seems as though he's going to explode any second. I can't think about that though, I need to focus on my course and the task ahead of me.

I turn him to the right and we pick up our posting trot. About halfway across the side I transition down to the sitting trot and then the walk. After a couple of strides, we pick up our left lead canter and head around the corner and down the side of the arena to position ourselves for the first jump.

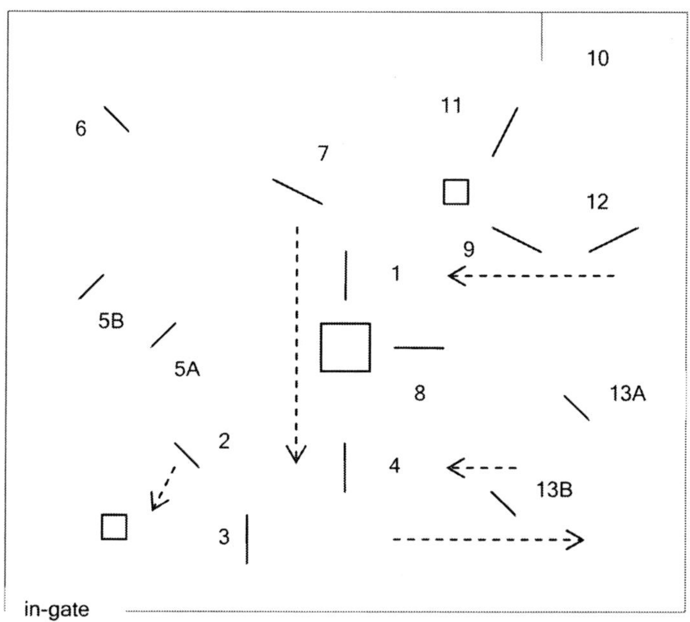

2007 Marshall & Sterling Children's Horse Medal Final
Round 1

Jay is already being fussy, attempting to flip his head as we canter around. Approaching the first jump, he seems to settle down a bit and focus. We get over the first two jumps well, but after we land and turn after the second jump to take the inside track to jump three, Jay decides to look at the scary green and white box monster on his right as we pass. He then thinks about running out on the third jump and drifts toward the right to the wall and the in-gate. There is no way I'm going to let that happen, so I pull his head around as hard as I can to the left, point him toward the jump, sit down, squeeze him with my legs, and get him over it. My leg barely misses hitting the right standard by mere inches.

Realizing that my chances of making the callback are getting slimmer by the second, I vow to get Jay through the rest of the course with no run outs or refusals even if I have to jump him from a walk. Several strides after the jump he decides to swap his lead. I immediately ask him to swap it back as we set up for the rollback to jump four. I had originally planned to take a track on the inside of jump 13B, but decide to go around it instead. I'm so focused on keeping him moving forward toward the jump, I end up getting left as he goes over.

We head toward jumps 5A and B on a bending line. Three strides out Jay thinks about running out, pulls back and swaps his lead, telling me "I don't think so."

My response is a very firm and definite, "Oh yes you will!"

I sit down in my seat and push him forward. He swaps his lead back one stride out and goes over. To my utter surprise, he ends up getting a really good distance and we're able to get through the second fence of the in-and-out without a problem. As we make the turn to jump six, Jay again wants to run out and drifts wide to the left causing me to have to pull him back hard to the right toward the jump to get him over.

He takes jumps seven, eight and nine well, but I realize I'm being very stiff in my upper body, especially my arms. As we come off jump nine for the turn to jump ten, I overcompensate and bend him too far to the right causing him to swap to his right lead. I then have to get the lead change to balance him for the approach to the next fence. Again as we near the jump, Jay thinks about ducking out and I have to push him forward.

My plan for jumps eleven and twelve had been to rollback tightly to take them at an angle, thereby making a straight line between the two. Since Jay is having a hard time focusing, we end up making a wide turn to the first fence which forces us to make an exaggerated bending line to the next one.

All I can think of now is that I just have to get us through the second in-and-out and we're done. Jay hesitates slightly right before the first fence and ends up pulling the rail with one of his back legs as he goes over. We land, take two strides and jump the last fence. It was by no means our prettiest or most graceful effort, but at least I got him over every single jump.

I walk out of the ring and am met by my mom and Kristine. At that moment I feel like crying; I'm so disappointed. My mom looks up at me and says, "Baby, you did the best you could with what you had. Under the circumstances, there's nothing to be upset about. You achieved your goals; you competed in your first national final and you got Jay over everything. I am so proud of you!"

I lean over so she can hug me.

Expecting a score in the 40's or low 50's based on previous rounds, I'm cautiously surprised when I think they announce that I scored a 62. Keith and Debbie are making their way toward us, so my mom asks them, "What did they just say Alyx's score was?"

Keith responds, "Sixty-two."

My mom turns back to me, "See it wasn't as bad as you thought it would be. I have to believe the judges gave you credit for getting Jay over everything. I'm sure they could tell that he wanted to duck out several times, but you refused to let him and kept on going."

Sitting atop Jay outside the ring, I remind myself there were a lot of riders throughout the weekend who'd received much lower scores than I did with horses that went around for them without any problem. Admittedly, I'm still disheartened by what has just occurred because I'd really wanted to do well, but my mom is right, I did achieve my goals.

My mom pats my leg and says she's proud of the fact that I persevered and didn't give up. She tells me she'll meet me back at the barn, then heads up the stairs and across the top of the berm to talk to our family and friends. Once she's out of sight, Jay and I begin the long walk back to the barn with Kristine.

Epilogue

Kristine was very supportive as we made our way across the showgrounds back to the barn; telling me I had done a great job, I'd become a lovely rider and how proud she was of me. Needless to say, I sincerely appreciated everything she said, I just wish she hadn't felt the need to make disparaging comments about Jay from the minute I'd exited the ring. Regardless of what had happened, Jay was still my partner and I loved him.

During the past three years we had consistently proven time and again that we could receive a top placing at any show. I had accomplished everything I'd set out to the previous September and Jay had been my trusted partner every step of the way. It didn't matter what anyone said, I couldn't have made it to the top of the standings or the Finals without him.

Once she arrived at the barn, my mom became the voice of understanding and reason. She reminded me that Jay had been relaxed and confident the two days we'd schooled in the Grand Prix ring and in the Hudson Equitation class. It was obvious something in his world changed that morning which adversely affected his behavior. We certainly couldn't change what happened, but we could learn from the experience.

As we had come to understand the puzzle that was Jay, we'd determined that he was not a horse that was comfortable with any type of change; he was definitely a creature of habit that liked routine. I certainly understood what Kristine was attempting to accomplish by sending him into the ring after hitting the rail and believed she had my best interests in mind. Unfortunately, it was a situation that caused Jay a great deal of anxiety. For over two years we'd followed the same procedures to prepare and school him at every show. He knew that toward the end of our warm-up we'd raise the jump higher and after he took it nicely a couple of times he was ready to go into the ring. I had to believe that if I had been able to take him over a jump no higher than 3'6" at least once more without issue, he would never have behaved as he had during our medal round.

Yes, our performance was disappointing, but I never shed a single tear about it and was back to my smiling, laughing self in a matter of minutes. As I untacked Jay, I realized that regardless of what had just occurred in the ring, we were still winners. The Final was one class, on one day; anything could, and did happen. Considering the circumstances and what we'd been through in the past, I was still extremely pleased with Jay. Although he had obviously been distressed, he'd listened to me and followed my directions throughout our round. I could sense his fear, insecurity and lack of confidence, yet I refused to let him give up and we got through the course together with no refusals or run outs.

Having achieved my goals for 2007, Jay and I plan to take several months off for a long overdue and well-deserved vacation from the show ring. In the interim I'll finally have some time to work with Riley. Like my mom I believe he has a great deal of untapped potential. With his natural talent and style for jumping, as well as his ability to learn new maneuvers quickly, I hope to be able to develop him into a competitive jumper and back-up equitation mount.

One thing that has been evident from the time Riley competed in his first show is he has a presence about him that attracts attention no matter where we go; it isn't just his size, it seems to be more about who he is. I find it quite entertaining when people approach us trying to determine his breeding. I've been asked if he's a Hanoverian, a Dutch Warmblood or an Oldenburg. I love the reactions when I tell people he is a Thoroughbred, Percheron, Arab cross. Every once in a while I'll even throw in the fact that he's a PMU foal, which is guaranteed to generate a bit of a shock.

Riley definitely has talent and with consistent training and experience I'm sure he'll develop into a top competitor. As with Jay, there are people who have already tried to discredit him by saying "he's too heavy to be a show horse" and "no judge will ever look at him." Yet even with his limited show experience, he's already proven those naysayers wrong. Only time will tell what level he can reach and what we will be able achieve together; Jay's and my accomplishments are a true testament to that statement.

As I look back and think about how very far Jay has come; from the out of shape pasture ornament that imagined horse eating monsters around every corner to the beautifully athletic show horse and partner with whom I've developed an irrevocable bond, I'm humbled by the fact that such a remarkable creature was so willing to embark on my journey with me. While there were many times he lacked confidence or was fearful of his surroundings, he placed his trust in me and followed wherever I led. Even when the obstacles we faced seemed insurmountable, his desire to please me overcame any trepidation or physical discomfort he may have felt. He repeatedly demonstrated he has a great deal heart and I have come to deeply appreciate his incredible spirit. I always knew there was a champion inside him, even when others expressed their doubts. Time and time again he proved I was right to have faith in him. Like Cheyenne, Riley and my beloved Bo, "Jaybird" has earned his permanent status and will always have a home with me.

While I may end up falling behind while we enjoy our time off, my goal for 2008 is to move up to 3'6" and earn some association and circuit year-end awards in the Equitation 15-17 division. With practice and experience, I hope to be able to qualify for the Maclay and USEF medal finals in 2009. As expected, I've already been told on numerous occasions that Jay will never be a 3'6" horse; but I know better. And with mom and dad there to support me along the way, there's no doubt in my mind that my dream of being able to successfully compete in the juniors will become a reality.

Realizing the competition at the upper levels of equitation is fierce, I would love to someday have the opportunity to work on a regular basis with Scott Hofstetter, Missy Clark, Don Stewart, or one of the country's other highly-respected trainers. For me, it would be an incredible honor to learn from any of them and be able to show under their tutelage. Although the ability to do so is probably outside of my reach, I will nevertheless forge ahead toward achieving my new goals. Whatever the future holds for us, I know Jay and I will be successful. There will never again be any doubt that Jay is, and always will be, my champion.

Glossary of Terms

Bascule – the form of a horse's body as they jump an obstacle. A horse with "good" bascule will have roundness to their form as they stretch their back and arc their body over a jump.

Canter – a three beat gait that is faster than a trot, but slower than a gallop. When riding on a circle the canter stride begins as the outside hind foot hits the ground for the first beat while the other three legs are in the air. During the second beat, the inside hind foot and outside front foot hit the ground simultaneously and the opposite legs are in the air. On the final beat, the inside front foot extends to hit the ground while the other three legs are in the air. This is followed by a moment when all four legs are off the ground before the next stride begins. The canter is the primary gait used when navigating a course of jumps.

Chip – jumping an obstacle from too close a distance.

Collection – the shortening of a horse's stride so that they shift their weight backwards for greater impulsion from the hindquarters, which allows them to become "lighter" on their front end.

Combination – two or more jumping obstacles set up as a line with no more than several strides between each of them.

Counter canter – when the horse's outside front leg extends to complete the third beat of the canter when riding on a circle; this is referred to as the wrong lead. In equitation classes riders may be asked to purposely ride on the counter canter.

Courtesy circle – upon entering the show ring, the transition from the walk to the trot to the canter on a circle to establish the horse's pace before approaching the first jump of a course. It is also used to transition down from the canter to the trot upon the completion of a course before exiting the show ring.

Fault – a penalty incurred in a jumper class for knocking down a pole or other element of a jumping obstacle, a disobedience by the horse (a refusal or run out), or for going over the time allowed.

Flying lead change or lead swap – when a horse changes from one lead to the other while all four legs are in the air between strides.

Flat or under saddle – classes that do not include any jumping. In equitation they are referred to as "on the flat" classes and in hunters they are "under saddle" classes. Riders can be asked to perform at the walk, trot, canter, counter canter, or hand gallop. They may also be asked to halt, reverse direction, perform a lead change, or back-up.

Frog – the tough, rubbery tissue found on the bottom of a horse's hoof that extends from the heel toward the toe to form a triangular shape. The frog acts as a shock absorber and aids in the circulation of blood flow through the legs.

Gallop – a four beat gait in which a horse can attain its fastest pace, reaching top speeds averaging 25 to 30 miles per hour. The movement at the gallop is very similar to the canter except that each foot hits the ground independently of the others, allowing for a longer stride and more ground covering pace.

Getting left – the failure of a rider to "fold" their upper body and follow the movement of the horse as it rises over a jump. When a rider "gets left" they are behind the horse's motion which causes their upper body to be pulled backwards in the saddle as the horse jumps.

Getting the distance – the "take-off" spot where the horse leaves the ground from the correct distance to jump an obstacle so that the effort appears even and smooth.

Hand gallop – a controlled gallop.

Hunt seat equitation – classes in which the rider is judged on their performance as they jump over fences or work on the flat with an emphasis on the correctness of their position in the saddle, the use of their hands, control of the horse, and overall riding style.

Children's Medal – an equitation class open to riders under the age of 18 in which competitors show over a course of at least eight jumps set at a height of 3'. Upon completion of a first round, the highest scoring riders return for a second round or "test" to determine the final placings.

Junior Medal – the highest and most competitive level of equitation classes open to riders under the age of 18 in which competitors show over a course of jumps 3'6" in height. The most prestigious of these classes are the ASPCA Maclay and USEF Medals.

Hunters – classes in which the horse is judged based on its performance; inclusive of its overall appearance, soundness, quality of movement, jumping form, and manners.

Children's Hunter – hunter classes open to riders under the age of 18 in which competitors show either over a course of jumps set at 3' or under saddle. In addition to the normal hunter judging criteria, an emphasis is placed on the suitability of the horse as a child's mount. The relation of the rider's size to that of the horse is also a consideration.

Handy hunter – a hunter class over fences that incorporates bending lines, roll backs, trot jumps, or other elements that test the horse's ability to smoothly and effortlessly navigate a challenging course.

Hunter Pleasure – an under saddle class in which the horse is judged on its movement, responsiveness to the rider, ability to maintain an even and controlled pace, as well as, its overall appearance. As the name implies, the horse should give the impression that it is enjoyable and easy to ride.

In and out – two jumping obstacles positioned with one stride between them.

Jumpers – classes in which horses and riders must navigate a course of jumps within a specified amount of time without accumulating any faults. The horse and rider with the fastest time and a clear round (with no faults) or with the fewest overall faults is declared the winner.

Power and Speed – a jumper class consisting of two parts; a power phase and a speed phase. The first half of the course is the power phase and it is not timed. If the horse and rider complete this phase without any faults, they continue riding over the second half of the course, which is the speed phase. This phase is timed and the horse and rider combination with the fastest time and least number of faults wins.

Lead – the front leg that is extended during the last beat of each canter stride. When cantering on a circle or in the show ring the inside leg should be the one extended; this is referred to as the correct lead. The horse will either be on their right lead if they are traveling clockwise or their left lead if they are traveling counter clockwise.

Line – two obstacles that must be jumped one after the other with a designated number of strides between them. The jumps can be set up as a straight or bending line.

Liverpool – a jumping obstacle with water underneath it.

Local show – shows not recognized by the United States Equestrian Federation. Most local hunter/jumper shows use the same judging criteria and class specifications as those established by the USEF.
Lunge – a method of training and exercising horses from the ground without a rider. The horse is asked to perform maneuvers on a circle, such as the walk, trot, and canter, while on a long rope or "lunge line." The individual working the horse stands in the center of the circle holding the lunge line as the horse moves around them.
Martingale – a form of equipment used to prevent a horse from throwing its head up. The standing martingale is a single leather strap attached to the underside of the bridle's noseband that is passed between the horse's front legs and connected to the girth. It is held in place by a strap attached around the base of the horse's neck. The running martingale consists of a leather strap attached to the girth between the front legs that splits into two pieces. Each piece has a metal ring on the end that the reins are passed through to provide leverage. Standing martingales are primarily used in hunter and equitation classes, while running martingales are used in jumpers. Martingales are not allowed in flat or under saddle classes.
Obstacles – the fences or jumps set up in hunter, jumper and equitation courses.
Oxer – two vertical jumps set apart from each other to create a spread obstacle.
One tempi – the changing of a horse's lead with each stride.
Over fences – classes in which the horse must jump over various types of obstacles.
Pull a rail – when the horse knocks down one or more poles of a jumping obstacle.
Quarter line – the unseen line that runs the length of the arena directly between the center line in the middle of the ring and the rail on the outside of the ring.
Rated show – a horse show recognized by the United States Equestrian Federation. These shows can be AA, A, B, or C rated based upon the amount of prize money being offered.
Refusal or run out – a horse's unwillingness to jump an obstacle. The horse may stop completely at the jump or "duck out" to either side in order to avoid it.

Roll back – a tight turn from one jump to the next within a course.
Scope – a horse's ability to easily and powerfully jump obstacles with little effort.
Sidepass – a lateral movement in which the horse moves sideways. While performing this maneuver, their outside legs will cross in front of their inside legs.
Soundness – the ability of a horse to effectively perform its intended job. For example, a hunter that is even mildly lame and unable to move smoothly and fluidly is not considered sound.
Standard – the structures used to hold up the poles, planks or other elements of a jumping obstacle.
Stride – the distance a horse travels to complete all phases of a gait. The average canter stride for a horse is 12 feet. When counting strides between jumps, 6 feet for the landing off the first jump and 6 feet for the take off to the second jump are included in the measurement. A line with a distance of 72 feet should be ridden in five 12-foot strides allowing for landing and take off. The distance between jumps may be set longer or shorter to test the rider's ability to adjust the length of their horse's stride.
Stride break – transitioning from one gait to another when not desired. This would occur if a rider was required to canter during a flat class and their horse slowed down to a trot for several strides before picking the canter back up again.
Surcingle – a strap made from leather, nylon or other synthetic material that fastens around the horse's girth behind their withers. A surcingle with metal rings on either side is typically used for lungeing. Training equipment, such as a neck stretcher or side reins, can be attached to the rings to help keep the horse in the proper position while they work.
Topline – the muscles that reach from the top of a horse's neck across their back to just past their hips. The topline should be gently defined with each body part appearing to flow smoothly from one to the next.
Thrush – an infection of a horse's hooves caused by exposure to excessive moisture, prolonged contact with manure, or reduced blood circulation to the frog due to improper trimming.
Trot – a two beat gait in which a horse's front leg moves forward at the same time the opposite back leg moves forward. This is the working gait of a horse and can be maintained for long periods of time. During

the posting or rising trot the rider moves up and down in the saddle with the horse's natural rhythm. At the sitting trot the horse's movement is slower and more collected so the rider can maintain their seat in the saddle.

Turn on the forehand – a lateral movement in which the horse turns its hindquarters in a circle to change direction while their front legs rotate in place.

Turn on the haunches – a lateral movement in which the horse turns its forehand (head, neck, shoulders, front legs) in a circle to change direction while their hindquarters rotate in place. For the turn on the haunches to be performed correctly, the horse must be moving forward at the walk before executing the turn.

Twitch – a device consisting of a wood or metal handle with a rope or chain loop around the end that is used to restrain a horse during stressful situations. The loop of the twitch is wrapped firmly around the horse's upper lip, which causes endorphins to be released in the brain and produces an overall calming effect. Twitching is considered a very humane form of restraint.

Vertical jump – an obstacle consisting of poles, planks, gates, or other elements that are each placed directly above one another to form an upright jump.

Printed in the United States
130223LV00002B/1/P

9 781593 305581